PRAISE FOR
DIVORCE DONE EASIER

This is an excellent boo‍ ... ting a divorce. The real-life exam‍ ... ‍ormation
easy to understand and e‍ ... done respectfully. Chapter 9 contai‍ ... ‍tion to the public
about the divorce options o‍ ... ‍ple are often not aware.
Hal D. Bartholomew, Collab‍...‍ative Attorney-Mediator, Fellow,
American Academy of Matrimonial Lawyers (AAML)

Divorce Done Easier by Carol Delzer is a must-read guide for anyone going through a divorce. It shows in clear, direct language the process of divorce and how to navigate it in a way that is respectful to your needs, the needs of your spouse and those of your children. The author is trained as both an attorney and a therapist and is able to guide you through the legal and emotional hurdles that often turn divorce into a protracted legal nightmare. You will find this book invaluable. **John O'Neal**, MD, author of *Handbook of Clinical Psychopharmacology*

I highly recommend Carol Delzer's new book *Divorce Done Easier* for all couples contemplating a divorce. In this book, Carol presents a hands-on practical, mindfulness-based approach to managing emotions, reactions and responses during divorce. She doesn't promise a stress-free path but she does predict a more peaceful and satisfactory outcome and future for anyone who chooses to follow the exercises in her book. As a Collaborative Divorce coach and Child Specialist, I will definitely be asking my clients to put these exercises into action throughout the course of the divorce proceedings. **Deni Deutsch Marshall**, Licensed Clinical Social Worker, Divorce Coach and Child Specialist

Carol Delzer has written a very accessible, empathetic book on a process that usually feels maze-like and downright inhumane. As she demonstrated with her first two books, *Collaborative Co-parenting* and *Positive Discipline for Single Parents,* it's as though you're chatting with a trusted (but firm) friend who wants to open doors and minds. *Divorce Done Easier* could easily be subtitled, "Let's be Grownups, Just This Once." It's a comprehensive, thoughtful work and I strongly recommend it. **Ed Goldman**, Daily columnist, Sacramento Business Journal

This book is comprehensive, holistic, and a culmination of sage wisdom and practical healing advice. It will motivate recovery as it is an excellent combination of legal and mental health supportive information. These real life illustrations will protect the kids and set the stage for movement and growth. I have found Carol's *Collaborative Co-parenting* to be so helpful with clients, they tend to "skip ahead" and read it all when their homework was just week 1 and 2. I look forward to adding this work to my present practice. **Timothy B. Rood**, MA, Licensed Marriage Family Therapist, Divorce Coach and Child Specialist

This book is a gift to anyone facing divorce! Carol Delzer has written a comprehensive primer about the divorce process and if you followed her suggestions, you can transition through this tumultuous life-changing event with less distress. Carol lives her life mindfully. I am grateful she is my colleague. **Linda Tell**, RN, Marriage Family Therapist, Child Specialist and Divorce Coach

Combining her years of experience as a therapist and attorney, Carol Delzer has written the most important book available on how to go through a difficult divorce in the most elegant way possible. If only this book and Carol's advice had been available during my divorce, it would have been better for the two of us, the kids, and our bank account. **Patrick McCallum**, Legislative Advocate for higher education and community colleges; founder of College and Corporate Brain Trust

Carol has written a book that will be extremely helpful for anyone going through a divorce. This book is a treasure filled with a wealth of knowledge and practical tools that people can use to make their divorce process more humane and less adversarial. Throughout the book, there are valuable tips and exercises to help the reader deal with change, communication, conflict and co-parenting. *Divorce Done Easier* is great information for people going through a divorce as well as family and friends who care about them. **Betsey Williams**, Licensed Marriage, Family Therapist, Collaborative Coach and Child Specialist

This book should be required reading in every divorce. Carol uses her expertise to clearly explain the legal process options and ways to grow through the real-life changes that divorce brings. This book includes essential strategies—about strong emotions, taking responsibility and effective communication—that can immediately help anyone make better decisions for a healthy future. **Kate Byrnes**, *MA*, Licensed Marriage and Family Therapist, Divorce Coach

From my perspective as a practicing family law attorney of over twenty years, this book is a must read—not only for those who may be considering divorce, but for those who have already committed to divorce. Carol Delzer helps readers understand the emotional processes that often lead to the decision to divorce and helps to identify and manage those processes. Readers will understand the transformational opportunities open to them with the insights from an experienced family law attorney and therapist, and will have the tools, communication techniques, and legal insights to help them through a difficult process; as well as alternatives to move through the divorce process in a respectful, cost-efficient, and less emotionally harmful manner. **Mark Johannessen**, JD, CFLS, Attorney-Mediator

Carol Delzer has charted a sensitive, compassionate and effective way for people who are divorcing to not only survive their divorce, but emerge wiser, less battered and more appreciative of their lives. She has provided guidance through what could otherwise be a destructive and more painful process. **Gary Friedman**, Attorney-Mediator, Author of *A Guide to Divorce Mediation* and *Challenging Conflict*; Cofounder and Trainer for Center for Understanding in Conflict

Divorce Done Easier can be the best gift you give yourself and your children to guide you through this life-changing event. Divorce can be so painful. However, this book can serve as a trusted friend to guide you through a respectful process that will help you heal the pain while learning skills for greater joy instead of bitterness. **Jane Nelsen**, EdD, author and co-author of the *Positive Discipline* Series

DIVORCE DONE EASIER

CAROL F. DELZER

Attorney-Mediator, Marriage Family Therapist

ISBN-13: 9781482328219
ISBN-10: 1482328216

Published by Family Law Center, Sacramento, California
Other books by Carol Delzer:
Collaborative Co-parenting for Divorcing Parents by Carol Delzer, 2009
Positive Discipline for Single Parents, co-authored by Carol Delzer, Jane Nelsen, Cheryl Erwin, 1995

www.Divorce DoneEasier.com
www.FamilyLawCenter.US
www.CollaborativeCoparenting.com

Available from Amazon.com

ACKNOWLEDGEMENTS

I have many people to thank for their support and inspiration for this book:

First my clients, for trusting me in their time of vulnerability and for all that I have learned from them.

I thank my staff and attorneys at Family Law Center for the support and time they helped me create so I could write this book.

Gary Friedman, Co-founder of the Center for Understanding in Conflict, who has been my trainer and mentor for over twenty years.

Hal Bartholomew, Collaborative Attorney-Mediator, who has been a visionary leader in the collaborative practice in California.

The members of Sacramento Collaborative Practice Group who have supported our vision: there are divorce options and you can get a divorce without going to court.

I am grateful for the continued spiritual inspiration I receive from Spiritual Life Center Unity Church in Sacramento and Spirit Rock Meditation Center in Marin.

Heather Estay, who helped transform my expertise into words the reader could easily understand.

Leslie Leggio, for final editing and walking the book through the publication process.

Last but not least, my daughter, Jessica, who is my friend and creative muse.

TABLE OF CONTENTS

Acknowledgements	**vii**
Introduction	**xiii**
Why should you trust me?	xiv
The Hard Way	xiv
A Different Way	xvi
What's the Difference?	xvii
CHAPTER 1 When Marriages Die	**1**
Broken Dreams, Unmet Expectations	3
Legally Irreconcilable	5
The Downside of No-fault Divorce	6
You Still Have Choice	7
About Time	9
A Timely Divorce	9
When to proceed?	10
CHAPTER 2 Tools for the Journey	**13**
Tool #1: Embracing Change—A Transformative Opportunity	14
Tool #2: Audit Your Attitude	14
Tool #3: Mindfulness	17
Tool #4: Stay in This Time Zone	20
Tool #5: Live in the Present, Plan for the Future	21

Tool #6: Go for the Goal 22

Tool #7: Let Go of the Past 24

Tool #8: Your Support System 26

CHAPTER 3 Cooperating with your Ex to Dissolve the Marriage 27

How Much?!? 28

How Dare You!?! 29

Old Dynamics 29

Respond Versus React 31

The Blame Game 32

Recapturing Self-Esteem 33

The Magic Key: Forgiveness 35

Your Choice 37

CHAPTER 4 Taking Charge of Emotions 39

Understanding Emotions 41

Major Emotions of Divorce 43

About Fear 43

About Anger 45

About Depression 46

Counseling 47

Emotional Mindfulness 47

Disarming your Emotional Triggers 48

Rehearsal Exercise 49

Heat of Battle Exercise—Push Pause 50

Challenging Your Self-Talk 51

Inquiry Exercise—Challenging Your Story 51

Seeing It Differently Exercise 52

CHAPTER 5 Build Your Foundation of Well-Being   **55**

   Get Moving   57

   Eat Well to Be Well   59

   Mood Food   60

CHAPTER 6 It's All about Communication   **63**

   Listening to Understand   63

   Listening Affirmations   68

   Communicating Your Needs   69

      Bottom Line: What is Your Intention?   70

      Non-Verbal Communication   71

      Tone   72

      The Words You Speak   73

      Take the War Out of Your Words   74

CHAPTER 7 From Conflict to Resolution   **77**

   Conflict Styles   78

   Why Collaborate?   83

   Mindful Inquiry   84

   Interest-Based Divorce Negotiation   86

   Decision-making Tools   89

CHAPTER 8 Co-Parenting   **93**

   From Marriage Partners to Parenting Partners   93

   Forming a Successful Parenting Partnership   94

   Talking to Children about Divorce   96

   Children Need Trust   .98

   Building Trust as Co-Parents   98

   Honoring Differences   99

   Do This for Your Children   101

CHAPTER 9 Divorce Process Options **103**

　　Mediation 104

　　Advantages of Mediation 105

　　Collaborative Divorce 107

　　Advantages of Collaborative Process 108

　　How the Collaborative Team Works 109

　　Settlement-Oriented Representation 110

　　Adversarial Divorce 112

　　Self-Representation 113

　　Divorce Options Workshop 114

　　Choosing the Right Professional Team 114

　　Finding the Right Mental-Health Professional 114

　　Finding the Right Legal Representation 115

　　Keeping Legal Costs Down 117

　　Your Most Important Decision 120

　　Conclusion 120

About the Author **123**

INTRODUCTION

Psychiatrists and psychotherapists will tell you that divorce is one of life's greatest stressors. Psychological studies put divorce right up there with death of a loved one or a critical illness in terms of the havoc it can wreak emotionally, financially and physically.

But you probably already know that or you wouldn't have picked up this book.

After over twenty years in practice where I have worked with countless divorcing couples, I can tell you that divorce does not have to be as traumatic and difficult as so many divorces turn out to be. I won't tell you that dissolving your marriage will be a walk in the park. That would be dishonest. But I will tell you that, with the right tools and the right approach, your divorce can be a positive launching pad for what's next in your life. You may not believe me just yet. You may just be praying that you make it through your divorce without devastating your financial security, traumatizing the children and losing your own sanity in the process. Divorce as "a positive launching pad" might feel like an impossibility, the stuff of fairy tales.

But can you at least entertain the possibility that your divorce doesn't have to be horrendous and painfully contentious? That maybe you and your soon-to-be ex can work together to create a more positive outcome for the two of you and your children? That you all can come out on the other side of this feeling okay about yourself and each other?

Depending on where you are, even that may seem a stretch. So I'll ask you to just keep reading.

Why should you trust me?

I've been there and done that—and even got the t-shirt! It was my own divorce many years ago that inspired me to find less brutal ways to dissolve a marriage both legally and emotionally. I became a family law attorney with a specialty in divorce mediation and collaborative practice. And, knowing that the psychological or emotional side of divorce is equally as important as the legal side, I earned my LMFT as a Licensed Marriage Family Therapist. (My website www.FamilyLawCenter.US contains a detailed Curriculum Vitae.)

I have helped over a thousand couples divorce and have witnessed the full gamut of financial circumstances, personality types, and causes for the separation, clients of all ages and ethnicities, and family dynamics. In 90% of these cases we were able to create a mutually acceptable dissolution through a process that was respectful, non-adversarial and much less expensive than so-called "normal" divorce proceedings. Usually in the beginning of the process, these clients were anxious and uncertain, struggling to figure out just how life would look after divorce. But by the time everything was finalized, the vast majority of them felt confident and empowered.

You can too.

Like my professional background, this book will focus on the emotional and psychological aspects of divorce as well as your options for the legal process. Why? Because, if you're in a rotten place emotionally, you cannot make good decisions. And if you make bad decisions, it will be tough for you to recover emotionally and financially from the dissolution. The two go hand in hand.

Let's begin with a couple of real-life examples (the stories are real, though I've changed names and identifying details to protect the confidentiality of the parties).

The Hard Way

Ted and Dana, both in their early forties, had been married for thirteen years and had three children. As a regional sales manager,

Ted did a considerable amount of traveling for his work while Dana was a very active stay-at-home mom.

Dana and Ted's relationship had been in trouble for several years but neither of them did anything to end the marriage due to concerns about the children. Ted's demanding travel schedule was also an issue; he didn't want to spend the little time he had at home bringing up difficult issues. Rather than a marriage, Dana and Ted were simply living parallel lives with little or no intimacy or communication.

Dana dealt with her misery by shopping. At first, she was able to cover her extra purchases within the income allotted for household expenses. But soon, Dana's shopping sprees took on a life of their own. She ran the family's credit cards up to their limits and applied for additional cards. She started hiding her purchases from Ted and, because she paid all the bills, she was able to hide their quickly growing debts from him for many months. But it all started to unravel when Dana was no longer able to pay the minimum amount due on all the credit cards. Creditors started making collection calls—and Ted happened to pick up one of those calls.

Ted demanded an explanation and Dana tearfully confessed. When Ted realized the extent of the problem, he became outraged and mistrustful. He decided to take action to protect himself and the family. Furious with Dana, Ted moved what remained of their joint savings account into an account in his name only. Also, without telling Dana, he closed the joint credit-card accounts, leaving Dana with minimal funds and no access to credit or money beyond her basic needs.

Dana was with the children when she first attempted to use her credit card and it was declined. She was surprised and embarrassed. She went home to discover that the savings account had been emptied and she was horrified. She telephoned Ted. He did not take her call. She heard nothing from him until the next day.

Instead of calling, Ted sent Dana an email telling her how angry he was that she had betrayed his trust. He also stated that the actions he was taking were to protect him and the children. Dana was beside herself with fear and anxiety which caused emotional turmoil for the children.

Ted had hired an aggressive divorce attorney who he thought would protect his interests. Later that day, Dana and the children responded to a knock on the door. The man standing there handed her a large envelope and said, "You are being sued for divorce and here are the papers. You have 30 days to respond." Dana closed the door and broke into tears in front of the children and told them that their daddy was deserting her and them.

The next day Dana borrowed enough money from her parents to obtain her own aggressive attorney and filed for full custody of the children as well as spousal and child support. Ted and Dana's divorce went on for two-and-a-half years and cost them tens of thousands of dollars. The emotional damage and destruction that was caused to both them and the children will take years, if ever, to repair.

A Different Way

John and Elizabeth, also in their forties, had been married for fourteen years and had two children. They had been in marriage counseling on and off for five years and had worked hard to work through their differences. They wanted to stay together for the children but it just wasn't working and they were both very unhappy.

During one counseling session, John confessed to having an affair with a woman from work. He told Elizabeth he had ended the affair, was deeply sorry and promised he would never be unfaithful again. But after doing the best she could for five years, Elizabeth said she just couldn't try anymore. She was done with the marriage and counseling, and the constant conflict was making her crazy. She felt that the differences between them were too great. The affair was the final straw, and she felt hurt and betrayed. John admitted that he had given up on ever having a happy marriage several months before but was staying for the sake of the children.

The couple's counselor had worked with them for several years. She acknowledged both of them for working hard on their relationship but agreed that it was probably time to consider coming apart. She asked them to consider using divorce mediation as a process to dissolve their marriage, explaining that divorce mediation would help them come to an equitable divorce that would serve everyone's best interest, especially the children's. The therapist recommended me as their attorney-mediator to mediate their divorce. Additionally, she recommended that each of them stay in counseling to deal with the emotional repercussions of John's affair so that it would not negatively impact their divorce process.

John and Elizabeth ended up divorcing through the mediation process. Through this process, the two of them were able to work together to create a co-parenting plan, sharing their children's time in a way that served the children's best interests. The children adjusted well and even seemed to thrive without the tension of their parents' differences and constant conflict in the household. John and Elizabeth were able to reach a fair and equitable financial agreement dividing their assets and debts. The process took less than six months to complete and saved them both emotionally and financially.

What's the Difference?

The two couples were quite similar in age, duration of marriage, family demographics and financial status. The circumstances of their "irreconcilable differences" were not the same. But, honestly? That wasn't what made one divorce devastating and the other empowering. The real difference was that John and Elizabeth: (a) had worked through some emotional issues within themselves individually and as a couple, (b) were dedicated to staying in respectful communication, even during this upsetting time, and (c) chose a legal process that would not set them up as adversaries.

Throughout this book, I will show you how you can do the same.

Chapter 1

When Marriages Die

Why do marriages fall apart? Bottom line: in the eyes of the law marriages end because of irreconcilable differences. Period. It doesn't matter if you and your spouse grew apart, or one of you betrayed the other, or you simply don't share the same core values and never really have. Whatever it is, at this point in the eyes of the law, it has become irreconcilable. An irreconcilable difference is any sort of difference where two parties *cannot* or *will* not change in order to come together.

As couples, most of us start out with differences but we assume we'll be able to work them out or they just aren't that important. We may even realize we don't know absolutely everything about the person we decided to marry, so we may discover differences we didn't know about. But we certainly didn't think we would have *irreconcilable* differences. If we did, none of us would have ever married in the first place!

Marriages start with differences we know about and differences we don't know about. Then, as time passes, yet another component is thrown in: change. What changes? Life itself changes and is ever changing. Our circumstances change. We have children, we make or lose money, we move closer to or away from family.

Our perspectives change. We become more or less conservative, more or less spiritually oriented. Our bodies change. Our attitudes change. Our hobbies, interests, careers, passions—almost everything about us changes. In fact, as John F. Kennedy once said, "Change is the law of life." Change is the one thing you can count on to be constant.

And change is good, right? You wouldn't want to stay frozen in time and remain the same person you were in your teens. Change is about growing and maturing and expanding our horizons. Sometimes, couples do this growing and expanding together. But sometimes the changes that two individuals go through lead them farther apart. Let's take a look at a specific case study.

Susan, an attorney in her mid-thirties, and Thomas, an accountant in his late thirties, met on the internet dating service, Match.com. After exchanging emails, they were both excited to meet. Their first coffee date was great! The physical attraction was strong, and they discovered they had much in common. They both played tennis, loved to travel, and even read the same books.

After a year of wonderful romance and exciting vacations together, Susan and Thomas married. They were both eager to start a family and had two children within the first four years of their marriage. They decided that Susan would leave the demanding schedule of her law practice and work from home designing websites so she had more flexibility to work around the children's schedules. Thomas took on the role of the main breadwinner in the family.

After eight years of marriage, Susan became depressed and began seeing a therapist. She knew she had a great husband and the children she'd always wanted, so she couldn't figure out why she was unhappy. She simply did not feel good about herself anymore. During therapy, Susan took stock of how much her life had changed after marriage. She had gained a lot of weight from having the children, and her work life was definitely not as exciting and fulfilling as her work as an attorney. She sorely missed being more physically active and having a regular work schedule with colleagues who stimulated her intellectually. Although Susan adored her children, being a stay-at-home mom did not give her the mental challenge she craved.

Thomas was working long hours to make up for the loss in Susan's income, and he felt constantly stressed. He was also starting to resent how much the relationship had changed. He didn't understand why Susan wouldn't get out and play tennis with him anymore, and he found himself less attracted to her. Not only had Susan gained weight, but she didn't pay as much attention to her appearance as she had in the beginning. She just didn't seem to care anymore. Their conversation was not fun and lively as it had been years before either. Susan seemed interested only in talking about the children or about household and financial duties she wanted him to handle.

Susan and Thomas began to have constant disagreements about anything and everything. Their arguments became bitter, filled with blame and contempt for one another. Finally, Susan decided to call it quits and told Thomas she wanted a divorce. She stated their differences were too much for her and she felt the marriage was irretrievable.

Does any of this sound familiar? Susan and Thomas started out as a very compatible couple and put together the life they thought they wanted. But as circumstances changed and each of them individually changed, it no longer worked. This is not that uncommon. Maybe, with more awareness and better communication, they could have recognized what was happening and made adjustments earlier—or maybe not. The point is that by the time they recognized they had issues, their differences had become irreconcilable.

Broken Dreams, Unmet Expectations

Most marriages begin with high expectations. Our weddings, whether large or small, were the public celebrations of this glorious new life of "happily ever after" we were about to enter.

Even wedding vows, besides setting contractual expectations for the relationship, proclaim our fervent dream that we will love and honor one another "until death do us part." In movies and fairy tales, couples always ride blissfully off into the sunset by the end of the story—and even the most cynical among us hope for the same for ourselves.

Some of our high marital expectations are conscious and some are not. A new bride might be clear that she expects her husband to be faithful and kind, but she may not recognize that her "perfect mate" is also supposed to be charming at family gatherings and buy her jewelry for her birthdays. A new groom may consciously expect his wife to be loyal and understanding, but he may not be conscious of his expectation that she initiate sex frequently and is a terrific budgeter. Of course, it's hard enough to meet someone's explicitly stated expectations. The ones that are hidden when even the person who has them doesn't realize they exist? Impossible!

Yet we're still disappointed when our conscious and unconscious expectations of our mate don't happen. Not only are we shocked and upset when our expectations aren't met, but we also attribute meaning to the fact that they aren't met. "If he really loved me, he would. . ." "If she really cared about me, she would. . ." Any of that sound familiar? We assume (mistakenly) that our partner understands our expectations and values the same things we do. So when expectations are not fulfilled, we see ourselves or our partner as lacking somehow, rather than recognizing (and maybe modifying) our original expectations.

So what were your expectations of marriage? Did you think that your spouse would satisfy all of your emotional needs? That, in your married life, sex would be frequent, spontaneous, and always gratifying? Did you believe the two of you would face every crisis as a strong team? That you would share household, financial, and child-rearing responsibilities equally?

Your expectations were not right or wrong. They just are what they are—and clearly identifying them may be a great asset for your next relationship. But for now, the disappointment of unmet expectations and broken dreams can be devastating and very painful. You may place a lot of blame on your spouse that he/she did not live up to your expectations or promises made. You may blame yourself and feel a lot of guilt that your marriage did not turn out to be "happily ever after." The truth is, more often than not, both parties contribute to the breakdown of a marriage. And how you deal with your feelings of pain and disappointment will have a tremendous impact on how difficult or reasonable the divorce process is for you.

Legally Irreconcilable

"Irreconcilable differences" is a legal term and the most common reason for granting a no-fault divorce. Some states use the terms irremediable breakdown, irretrievable breakdown, or incompatibility, but basically they all mean the same thing: *The existence of significant differences between a married couple that are so great and beyond resolution as to make the marriage unworkable, and for which the law permits a divorce.*

Most states have some form of no-fault divorce now, though some states require extensive waiting periods before granting the final dissolution of marriage. (Your divorce will be governed by laws of the state within which you and your spouse live.) No-fault divorces were created to avoid the messy, painful and expensive process of establishing that one person was to blame or totally responsible for the breakup. Prior to no-fault divorces, divorce was handled as a breach of contract. So even in cases where the separation was amicable and mutual, someone had to be painted as the bad guy in front of a judge. No-fault divorce removes that necessity (though some divorcing parties still opt for various reasons to go the "breach of marital contract" route). Judges routinely grant a divorce as long as the spouse seeking the dissolution states that the couple has irreconcilable differences. By law, if one party says the marriage is irretrievable and refuses to reconcile, then such differences are proven to exist. As a practical matter, courts seldom even inquire into why the couple is choosing to divorce in no-fault cases. Surprisingly, this has a downside.

The Downside of No-fault Divorce

Though no-fault divorce has definitely helped many couples avoid the nastiness of proving that one party has breached the marital contract, many of my clients have a difficult time coming to terms with the concept of "no-fault" in the breakdown of the marriage. "Of course, there was fault! If he hadn't done X, Y, Z, we'd be fine!" "If only she had done X, Y, Z, we would still be together!" Something or someone had to be *wrong* for this breakup to happen.

Even when the divorcing spouses are not determined to place blame on the other, they still feel a natural impulse to question *why* and *how* it happened. As human beings, we're wired for survival. When something happens that harms or hurts us, we instinctually try to figure it out so we can avoid that pain in the future. We're not just curious—we're almost driven to come up with a way to understand the situation.

And once we think we have it figured out, it feels equally important to tell others about it. To "get it off our chest." To "tell our side of the story." To "explain how it all happened." To "have their day in court," even if they settle outside of the courtroom. It is common to feel this strong need to explain why the marriage failed. Many of my clients can't come to closure or complete their divorce without expressing what they feel is true about the situation.

In my experience, if a spouse needs to talk about the history of the marriage breakdown and isn't given the chance to do so, the divorce process can become prolonged or adversarial. Because they haven't had an opportunity to discuss why the marriage ended and their experience of what went wrong, frustration builds up. Unfortunately, they often use the divorce process itself to work through this frustration, creating unnecessary roadblocks, confusion, delays and pain.

In Chapters 4 and 6, I'll talk about ways to express these feelings and how to use them to your benefit, not your detriment. You will learn how you can use the story of "what happened" to understand something about yourself and life in general. Doing this may seem a little farfetched right now. But I will give you illustrations of how staying mired in the blame game and reliving all of the hurts and disappointments will get you nowhere, except to make the divorce process more difficult and expensive.

You Still Have Choice

Despite the fact that you have come to the point where your differences, whatever they are, are irreconcilable, you still have a lot of choice in what happens next. The choice to "live happily ever after" with your current spouse may not still be an option. However, you still have a myriad of choices that can reduce the stress of your divorce and create a positive foundation for your future and that of your children.

Initially, it may feel like the divorce process has a life of its own, that you are skidding down a slippery slope and you can't find the brakes. You may feel powerless and out of control—but you aren't. Throughout this book, we'll talk about the choices you have within the divorce process and how to manage these choices so they don't manage and control you. We'll talk about how to regain your own power *without* disempowering your spouse. The decisions made during your divorce can be *your* choice.

You always have choice. Up to this point, you may have felt that life just happens and you have no control over it. But the opportunity to choose in every moment is as integral a part of life as is breathing. The truth is, even when you cannot control circumstances, you always have the choice of how you react to the people and situations in your life. When life hits the fan, you

always have the choice to learn and grow from it or become em-
bittered by it. You always have the ability to choose whether you'll
make decisions from a calm, empowered place or an angry, hurt
reactive place (we'll discuss how to make empowering decisions
in Chapter 4).

No matter how brilliant or how self-destructive your choices
may have been in the past, you can choose to do it differently going forward. Your history and the history of your marriage do *not*
predetermine your future. Reflecting on choices you made in the
past is helpful because you can learn from it, but it is not helpful
if you use it to beat yourself up. Honestly? Most of us do the best
we can at any point in time given who we are and what we know.
Maybe your past decision-making was not perfect, but this is your
opportunity to do it better to pave a path for an easier future for
you and your children to enjoy.

In Chapter 2, we'll explore how and why you made the
choices you did in the past. The choices you have made have
brought you to where you are today and the life you lived up to
this point. Maybe you chose to make choices arbitrarily without
first gathering all the information needed. Maybe you made
decisions in the heat of emotion that would probably have been
better if left for some other day. As we'll discuss in Chapters 2
and 3, there are better ways. Learning when, how and why to
make decisions may be the most important education you'll receive from this book.

Learning to make decisions from choice and being active
within the decision-making process is certainly more empowering than simply allowing others to choose for you. You can
learn to inquire neutrally and consider other people's choices
and propositions without necessarily agreeing with them. Even
if the two of you have not made positive decisions together in
the past, you can do so during your divorce. And it is critical
that you do because the sum total of the choices you make during this time will determine how easy or difficult your divorce
will be.

About Time

Unfortunately in a divorce, the time when you feel least capable of making good decisions is when you have to make them. There is a slice of time at the end of a marriage when you have to make the critical choice about how you will proceed with the dissolution. During this slice of time, the choices that are made about the divorcing process will have a huge impact on you, your children and your relationship with your future ex-spouse for several years, and maybe a lifetime. Choices such as:

> Who will depart and who will remain in the home?
>
> What type of legal/financial/emotional help will you seek?
>
> What form of divorce will you use (mediation, collaborative or adversarial attorneys, etc.?
>
> How will you handle financial and family issues until the settlement is final?
>
> How will you tell your children, your family, and your friends that you are divorcing?

A Timely Divorce

Even the decision of when to proceed with the divorce will create very different choices and outcomes. When a couple can communicate well enough at the time of breakup to make decisions together respectfully and cooperatively, they are in the best frame of mind to proceed. However, if emotions are still running high and a couple's communication is so mired in conflict that they can't make even simple decisions together, they usually benefit by completing the necessary temporary agreements initially and waiting a reasonable time to tackle the more complex, difficult and permanent decisions of the divorce. Time often heals wounds and soothes frayed nerves. Allowing a reasonable time before proceeding with all the details and decisions within a divorce can be very healing, reduce stress and allow for the best results and possibilities to emerge. Even if you and your spouse cannot communicate or you think you will *never* be able to work together or communicate, keep reading. You will find good solid advice in chapters ahead that will make your divorce easier.

This critical slice of time and choices made reminds me of the movie, *Sliding Doors*. Gwyneth Paltrow plays a woman whose boyfriend (unbeknownst to her) is having an affair. Gwyneth is fired from her job early one morning and heads home. At this point, the story splits into two different realities. In one, she catches her train home and finds her boyfriend in bed with the other woman. In the second reality, she misses the train and, by the time she gets home, her boyfriend's mistress is gone. The two stories continue from there, showing how her life proceeds along the two separate life paths based on catching or missing that train.

Choices you make in the initial phases of your divorce will lead you to very different experiences. Obviously, you are not making these choices alone. The two of you are determining the course of your divorce together, which can sometimes give you a feeling of powerlessness. In Chapter 7, we'll discuss how you alone can effect change, and restore balance of power in the divorce process, without giving up any of your legal rights.

When to proceed?

Timing can mean everything to a divorce process, a point that I constantly emphasize to my clients. It is critical to honor and respect each other's individual timing in moving through the divorce. Being aware of what each person needs and not trying to go faster than the slowest spouse can reasonably move will make a world of difference. In my experience, it is the best environment for moving a divorce along at the couple's pace, not the pace set by the courts or someone else. To move any faster than the slowest party can reasonably move in a divorce may push the couple into becoming resistant and adversarial, which is not an ideal direction for any divorcing couple.

I recently worked with a couple who met with me four times in mediation over an eight-month period without starting the filing for their divorce. They gathered information, worked together to understand the mediation process, and shared the details of their assets and debts. During the fourth visit, I asked if they were ready for me to file the divorce commencement documents to open the case with the court. The husband responded that he was leaving the timing up to his wife. The husband was the one who decided to end the 27-year marriage, and his wife was still distraught. He was sensitive to her feelings, so gave her the time she needed to emotionally prepare herself for the divorce. I was impressed with the respect and communication they exhibited, proceeding at a pace that honored them both. When, after nine months, the wife was ready to proceed, their divorce went smoothly and was completed in a short period of time.

I always ask my clients, "Whose decision was it to end the marriage?" This often opens up the discussion of timing for each spouse and how best to move forward. The person who makes the decision to end the divorce is often referred to as the "leavor." The spouse who did not make the decision to end the marriage is referred to as the "leavee." Psychological studies show the leavor is often 9-18 months further along emotionally than the leavee. I have seen a wide variation in this timing, and I have also noticed that males seem to recover faster as the one who did *not* decide to end the marriage than females in that situation.

If you were not the one who decided to end the marriage, you may still be dealing with the disappointment of the ending of the marriage and are not ready to be rushed into making decisions about your future. When we feel rushed or pushed into something, our normal human reaction is to resist. When resistance happens in the divorcing process, it increases conflict and adversarial positioning, eventually leading to decisions being settled by the court. When divorcing spouses take their fear and resistance to court, it may become the place to cathartically work through their personal emotional lack of readiness. But it's a shame that hundreds of thousands of dollars are spent because one spouse is in a hurry to move forward, when all that was really needed was just a little more time. It is also a shame to see one spouse unreasonably delay the process because they did not have the tools to prepare themselves. Spouses who are willing to be patient, pacing the divorce to respect both parties' needs, will save not only thousands of dollars, but also avoid additional pain and conflict.

Throughout this book, we'll discuss how to prepare yourself emotionally and practically to move forward in your divorce in a timely manner and how to ask for the time you need for this preparation.

Chapter 2

Tools for the Journey

As Lao Tzu famously said, "The journey of a thousand miles begins with one step." I can't take that step for you, but I do have a number of tools that will make your journey easier and less painful while producing more positive outcomes for you and your family. These tools are not legal strategies or recommendations about how to divide your assets. They're more powerful than that. The tools offered in this chapter and throughout the book focus on your most important asset during this process: you and your emotional and mental capacities. You have a genius and power that for many people is usually only tapped in times of crisis. Throughout this book and especially in this chapter, I want to make sure you have the tools to tap into that power. As A.A. Milne put it, "Promise me you'll always remember: You're braver than you believe, and stronger than you seem, and smarter than you think."

Tool #1: Embracing Change—A Transformative Opportunity

As we discussed earlier, life is all about change. Sometimes it is welcome, but other times it's terrifying. Many of us are adamantly averse to any type of change. Whether our current circumstances are good or not good, we would still prefer to keep things the way they are, within our comfort zone. People even stress over seemingly positive changes such as financial windfalls or career promotions. The life we *know* just seems safer than that big *unknown* out there.

Getting divorced and becoming single usually fall into the not-so-welcome change category. The physical, emotional and financial adjustments of divorce can be overwhelming. Right now, your life may seem broken beyond repair. It may be hard to imagine, but over the years I've seen that this can be a positive turning point in a person's life. Besides, right now, you don't really have the option to keep everything the same, do you? So rather than resist the changes coming, let's learn to be good at moving through them!

People who are good with change embrace it. They don't waste their time kicking and screaming about it, whining to their friends or complaining to their co-workers. Instead, they focus on asking questions like, "What's next?" or "How can I grow from this experience?" or "How can I make this change as positive as it can be?"

If you're willing to fully embrace the changes that your divorce will bring to the best of your ability, you'll have the opportunity to create a rewarding new life for yourself and your family. So take a deep breath, and let's get started.

Tool #2: Audit Your Attitude

More than anything else, the one attribute that separates people who adjust well to change and those who do not is attitude. Change is inevitable, but you have the choice to make this change better or worse for yourself. Highly successful people are always looking for opportunities to change because change is growth. Here are some ways you can shift your own attitude so that it serves you better:

Alternative Attitude Statements: Ask yourself, "What is my current attitude about the changes because of this divorce?" Be honest with yourself. Do you feel fearful? Overwhelmed? Resentful that you have to make these changes? Sit down and make a list, putting all of your current attitudes into statements such as: "Change stinks." "My life will never be as good as it was." "I can't handle all of these problems." Leave a few spaces between each statement. If you have any positive attitudes about this change, great! Write those down too.

Now, looking at your list, what are some *different* attitudes, new ways of thinking and feeling, you can adopt? What attitudes would be more helpful and feel better? These alternate attitudes may not come to you immediately. Think about people you know who are great with change. How would they think about this? Imagine yourself feeling benefitted from this change. What would you be saying to yourself and to people around you?

Take each statement that reflects your current attitude and write an alternative statement. For example, you might counter "Change stinks" with "Change rocks!" How about switching from "My life will never be as good" to "My life can be even better." Maybe "I can't handle all these problems" can become "I'm fully ready to go on this adventure!"

I know that your alternate statements may seem phony at first, a Pollyanna wishful thinking kind of thing. But try saying your alternate statements a few times. Stand up straight and take a deep breath as you say them. Don't you feel a little lighter, clearer, more powerful? Doesn't it feel that you could make better decisions and interact with others more effectively with that attitude?

If you are feeling stuck trying to come up with alternative statements, here are a few to try on: "I have everything I need to move forward positively." "I am fully capable of handling whatever comes to me." "I am entering a new chapter of my life, a new adventure." "Others have made positive changes after divorce and so can I." "I will grow stronger, more aware and more capable through these changes." "I am surrounded by people who love me and care about me." "This divorce will be a positive transformation for me." "I have the energy and resources I need." "I know that when one door closes another one opens." "I know I can and I will succeed."

Watch Your Language: Attitude is reflected, and actually gets embedded, by the language we use to ourselves and others. Notice how you currently talk about your divorce and the changes it is creating. Are you using words like "problem," "difficult," "worried," or "impossible?" Think about it. If you keep telling yourself and others that your situation is "impossible" or "overwhelming," what does that do to your ability to move forward? It makes you feel less capable and powerful, doesn't it? Though it may not seem like much, changing the very words you use can have a big effect on how empowered you feel.

Years ago, success coaches started having us use "challenge" to replace "obstacle" or "problem." Why? Because a challenge can be fun. When you meet a challenge you feel heroic, brave, creative. A challenge takes you to the next level. Handling "problems" on the other hand is a burden. "Problems" means something is wrong and you have to fix it just to get back to normal. Can you feel the difference? Pay attention to your internal and external language. It may feel awkward at first, but catch yourself when you use negative words and start substituting more empowering ones.

Will you immediately experience a 180-degree shift in your attitude through these exercises? Probably not. But you don't need 180 degrees. Even small shifts will help you embrace the changes of the divorce process and beyond. Take small steps if you have to. If you're starting with, "I can't possibly handle this!" your new statement doesn't have to be "I am awesomely brilliant and extraordinarily powerful and I can handle anything!" You may want to start with, "I've handled challenges in the past and I'm pretty sure I can handle this one." As Oprah Winfrey put it, "The greatest discovery of all time is that a person can change his future by merely changing his attitude."

Tool #3: Mindfulness

What is mindfulness? Originally a practice in Buddhism, mindfulness was adopted by Western psychologists as an effective therapeutic technique. In modern psychology as well as Buddhism, mindfulness means to bring your total attention to the present moment. To be mindful is to purposefully pay attention to this moment with all its thoughts, feelings and sensations *without* judgment of right or wrong. Everything is accepted just as it is.

The nature of mindfulness is to become more present to your life experience and more alive in the moment, more intentionally responsive and less reactive. In a mindful state, you let go of pre-conceived notions about yourself and others; you simply experience *what is* in the present moment. You open yourself to a greater sense of creativity and connectedness.

Mindfulness basically means awareness. Now more than any other time, it is important to be fully aware of what is going on. With the stress of your marriage breakup and changes in your life, it may feel more challenging to be aware and mindful. There are many things you can do to change your unawareness to a more mindful awareness.

Mindfulness has a way of sounding complicated. It is anything but. It is as simple as paying attention in the moment to information you receive *without judging it.* The minute you begin to judge information you receive, your mind is entangled in *judgment* and is not fully present to receive the information. You receive only *partial, inaccurate* information because you're distracted by your judgments and reactions.

For example, many couples have a dynamic of splitting the responsibilities. So you may enter into the divorce process not having information about your spouse's responsibilities. You may not have financial details or may lack information about the children. It's important that both of you have full information about everything involved in the settlement. But often, as information is revealed, one partner or the other becomes reactive or overwhelmed. One spouse may feel overwhelmed because they do not understand the financial aspects of their marriage while the other spouse may feel angry about the additional responsibilities they will have with the children. Our anxiousness takes on a life of its own, little problems become big problems and then grow to even bigger problems. Being mindful is critical in order to continually process new information.

By using mindfulness, you can be fully present. You receive all of the information you need. You are able to respond rather than react. You *consciously choose* rather than make choices on autopilot or by default. You can listen more deeply and express yourself more authentically. Mindfulness is one of the best tools you can use for any of life's challenges.

Because I believe that mindfulness is so powerful and helpful, I will refer to it throughout this book. But to get you started, here are a few tips and exercises to train yourself to become more mindful:

1. Practice mindfulness during routine activities. Try bringing awareness to your daily activities that you may currently be doing on autopilot. For instance, try being mindful as you do the grocery shopping. Pay attention to details in the store and be really observant. Like an explorer discovering a new land, seek to leave the store with information that has always been there but you never noticed before. Notice colors throughout the store, the check stands, clerks, shopping carts. Give your full attention to products, the color and smell, the detail of each product. Without judging "good, bad" or "what I like, or what I don't like," simply observe all the grocery store has to offer.

2. Practice being mindful first thing in the morning. Set the tone for your day. As you wake up, notice your surroundings. Take in the colors, smell, texture and experience of your bedroom. Notice how you move from your bed to beginning your day. Don't judge, *observe*. Practicing mindfulness first thing in the morning helps set your nervous

system for the rest of the day, increasing the possibility of other mindful moments throughout your day.

3. Build your mindfulness ability. Keep your practice times relatively short when you begin. Your brain will respond to being attentive to information for short periods of time at first. When you start, set a period of time aside where you commit to being mindful with information for 15 minutes three times a day. After one week of doing the practice regularly for 15 minutes, increase it to 30 minutes twice a day. After one month, increase your practice to one hour at least once a day. You are preparing yourself to be mindful for when you are in meetings about your divorce that will often last between one to two hours.

4. Practice mindfulness while you wait. In our fast-paced lives, waiting is a big source of frustration—whether you're waiting in line or stuck in traffic. But while it might seem like a nuisance, waiting is actually an opportunity for mindfulness. It is also one of the best opportunities you can use to begin noticing information about other people. While you're waiting, bring your attention to the people around you. Notice if they appear frustrated, sad, happy, easy-going or uptight. Notice their facial expressions and their body posture. Practicing this will be of great help to you as you go through the divorce. Learning how to read body language is being mindful, paying attention, and being committed to practice.

5. Use an affirmation when your attention starts to drift away from listening for information. Whisper a silent affirmation to yourself and use it as a reminder to turn your attention back to the information at hand, for instance, "I am aware, I am listening, I am free of judgment and fear."

6. Follow a good plan like you follow your goals: do not run on automatic pilot, be consciously applying mindfulness with continuous effort.

7. Think about what you want to say, how you want to say it, and how what you say will impact the listener. If you have

a chance, write it down first. Or ask to take a break so you have time to think through what you want to say before you say it. You can also wait until you have had the time to work with a coach or talk to a professional about how to express what you need to say. This is Mindful Speech.

8. Mindfulness is about being reasonable and just. Don't unreasonably withhold an agreement. Remember agreements beget agreements. Being reasonable and just also extends to yourself. There is no need to agree to anything until you have had the time to determine its reasonableness for you. Be mindful in reaching agreements.

Mindfulness is not a luxury—it is a practice that trains your brain to be more efficient and better integrated, with improved focus and less distractibility. It minimizes stress and even helps you become your best self. There is now an abundance of neuroscience research to support that mindfulness practice helps our brains be more integrated, so your everyday activities, thoughts, attitudes and perceptions are more aware. The best way to become more mindful is through learning to meditate. There will be a further discussion on meditation in Chapter 5.

Tool #4: Stay in This Time Zone

As we discussed earlier, when a marriage falls apart, it is human nature to look back and ask, "What the heck happened?" It's a healthy process to delve back into the past when you use it to learn and grow. But it is not healthy to take up residence there! After you've gleaned the lessons that your history can teach you, rehashing it over and over simply saps your energy.

Can you change what happened in the past? No. Can you make the past different or better? No. Can you erase what you said or plug in what you should have said? No. Can you undo the decisions or choices you made? Nope. The only place you can make things better is in the *present* to lead toward a more positive future. Put your focus and energy on the here and now. Ask yourself,

"What can I do or say *right now* to feel or interact or communicate or make decisions better?" As Buddha said, "No matter how hard the past, you can always begin again."

And though it is good to look forward, you don't want to operate from there either. You may be anticipating a bright future or dreading an unknown one, but the only place you can really affect it is *now*. Your future will be determined by what you do, say and choose *right now*.

Often in the initial phases of a divorce process, my clients tell me that they simply don't *like* the present. Maybe they had to leave a beautiful home to live in a tiny apartment. Maybe they're having trouble handling the bills or stressing about their children's emotional upheaval. Maybe they've lost friends or connection to family members that were important to them. I fully understand that. But dwelling in the past or dreaming of the future will not help you feel empowered. Staying in the present, doing whatever small thing you can do *now* for yourself and your family, will give you a greater sense of purpose and stability. If there's an uncomfortable circumstance in your present that you can fix, fix it. Get that haircut, spruce up your new living space, start a workout program, take up a new hobby or volunteer in your children's schools or programs. But if there are things in your present over which you have no control, accept them and let them go.

Remaining in the present can be tricky. But if you stay aware and pull yourself back into your current "time zone" when you drift off, you will reap great benefits, feel much more capable to do what needs doing, and have a much easier time throughout the entire divorce process. As author Denis Waitley says, "Learn from the past; set vivid, detailed goals for the future; and live in the only moment over which you have control: now."

Tool #5: Live in the Present, Plan for the Future

Okay, as Yogi Berra said, "The future ain't what it used to be!" Consciously or unconsciously, you probably had a future mapped out based on your marriage. You knew where you would live and had ideas about the when and where of your retirement. Maybe you had vacations planned or trips to visit colleges for your kids. Perhaps you had visions of being grandparents together. But now all of that has come undone. Much of the pain of divorcing is that the future you envisioned disappears. It feels like a death of sorts, doesn't it?

Take a deep breath and acknowledge that the future you had in the past is gone. Honestly, it wasn't the only possible future for you, was it? What if you had not met your spouse or had married someone else? What if you had chosen a different occupation or had injured yourself in an accident? We all have crossroads in life that, depending on the choices we make, lead us to a different future. Right now, you're at another crossroad. One path is no longer available to you but several others are.

Often, when clients begin this process of looking into their new future, the outlook seems pretty bleak. They are still attached to that old future and what they've lost. As Alexander Graham Bell said over a century ago, "When one door closes, another opens, but we often look so long and so regretfully upon the closed door that we do not see the one that has opened for us."

Rather than focusing on what *isn't*, spend some time investigating what *could be*. Get curious. What are the possibilities? What could be next for you? In doing this, you'll want to stay open and loose. Imagine what is *possible*, not what (based on your current state and circumstances) is *probable*. Think big for yourself and your children. Raise the bar. Help your children create a new vision for their future as well. Though you definitely want to operate in the present, having a big, juicy vision of the future will be inspiring. It will challenge you to move beyond mere coping and surviving to living fully again.

Tool #6: Go for the Goal

Right now, it may seem exhausting to even think about setting goals! You might feel overwhelmed just trying to handle your day-to-day tasks. Adding a goal on top of that? Not gonna happen! But the truth is that goals, when done properly, actually energize us rather than expend energy. Just like a vision inspires us, well-structured goals activate all of our cylinders and get us moving again. "Coping" and "figuring out how to get through another day" will sap our energy, but goals refuel and refresh us.

Though goals are things that you accomplish, they are not to-do lists. And though goals should be a stretch for you, they are not as broad as your visions and dreams. For example, "I am healthy, slim and fit, loving my body" is a vision. "Go to the gym" is a task for your to-do list. But a goal is, "By June 30th, I am 15 pounds lighter and have developed a regular routine of working out 3-4 times per week." Or, "I consistently eat four servings of vegetables every day."

You may or may not be familiar with the science of goals. As Zig Ziglar once said, "A goal properly set is halfway reached." So here are a few characteristics of effective goal setting:

1. Measurable: Your goal must be something that you can measure so you will know when you have accomplished it. "Slimmer" is not a goal. "Size 8" is.

2. Set in Time: You need a specific "by when" for your goals. Without a deadline, it's much too easy to put off doing what needs to be done!

3. Present Tense: When you write your goals, experts say to put them in present tense, for instance "I am" rather than "I will" or "I want…." Why? Because your unconscious mind (which is a great asset in achieving goals!) takes you literally. If you say, "I will be this and that," your unconscious mind assumes that the goal is always beyond the present time.

4. A Stretch: Good goals help you expand and grow. Don't you feel great when you've accomplished something that is just a bit beyond what you've ever done before? This sense of being challenged is part of what makes goals energizing.

5. Realistic: If you have never run in your life, participating in a marathon that is three weeks away is not realistic. A goal that is too big of a stretch can be discouraging and stressful rather than energizing and enjoyable. Besides, your unconscious mind will know if your goal is too far out there and it will sabotage your efforts.

6. Personal: By this I mean that the goal, like your vision for the future, has to be something that is important to *you*. Other people may have ideas about what we should be or should want, but you're the one living your life, right? Make sure that you aren't setting your goals for your mother or the Joneses next door. Good goals are focused on what makes *you* feel fulfilled and happy.

What should you set goals about? In some ways, it doesn't matter. Just the act of setting a goal and moving toward it will make you feel better about yourself, more confident, and more capable—all qualities that are important as you proceed through the divorce process.

Tool #7: Let Go of the Past

We've discussed staying in the present and looking toward the future. Because attachment to the past is such a big stumbling block, it is worth exploring at more depth. During the divorce process, it is critical to thoroughly let go of the past as quickly as possible. If you don't, your decisions and choices will be colored by whatever hurt, anger, resentment, disappointment, and humiliation you still cling to.

Arrgh! This may not even seem possible just yet! However, the sooner you step into the process of letting go of all that negativity, the sooner you will return to your capable, loving, rational, creative, powerful and positive self. Isn't *that* the person who should be making all the important choices before you? Do you really want that crazy, bitter, reactive self to make decisions that will affect you and your children for many years to come? Do you want that resentful, vengeful self to undermine all the good you could do in this process?

While letting go of the past is important for the divorce process, letting go of all its pain is important to your own healing as well. Letting go of the past doesn't mean simply telling yourself to get over your emotions and get on with it. It doesn't mean that you should pretend your relationship never happened or that you're not hurting when, in fact, you are. What it *does* mean is learning to live each day in the present without constantly letting negative emotions such as blame, anger, and resentment run your life. It means processing through the pain in whatever way works for you, so that you come out on the other end feeling whole and complete.

During this critical time, many of my clients have benefitted from counseling or working with a divorce coach. They've picked up books (like this one!) to get thoughtful advice from people who have traveled this road before them. Whatever you choose, make this letting go process a priority. It will benefit you more than just about anything else you do. And to assist with this, try saying these affirmations (and others that come to you) aloud, breathing deeply as you do:

- I let go of resentment.

- I let go of anger.

- I let go of humiliation.

- I let go of fear.

- I let go of disappointment.

- I let go of past conflicts.

- I let go of emotional wounds.

- I let go of blame.

- I let go of lashing out.

- I let go of what might have been.

- I let go of the past.

Tool #8: Your Support System

We'll discuss how to build your professional support network in Chapter 9, but here, let's talk about your personal support. These are the friends and family who can help pick you up when you're down, act as good sounding boards for your issues and ideas, and encourage you as you move forward with your life. Optimally, these people believe in you, your capabilities and potential. They are the cheerleaders, not the naysayers. They care more about supporting your present and future than rehashing your past.

Do you have such a network? Many of my clients did not initially have one when they came to see me. Unfortunately, it is not uncommon for couples to form a tight unit and ignore the friends they had when they were single. Or they build a network of couples as friends and during a divorce these friends may take sides or feel uncomfortable interacting with you separately.

I strongly urge you to not try to go it alone. If you don't currently have a good positive network of friends and family, put some effort into developing one. Invite the mother of your child's playmate to lunch. Meet people by doing activities you enjoy. Join support groups or a spiritual community of your choice. Building a network of supportive friends, or even just one supportive relationship, can be vital to your wellbeing. The more people you have in your life, the more likely you are to have truly supportive relationships with at least one of them. Some people give off positive energy that makes you feel good. Others give off negative energy that is draining. Pay attention to your intuition to find a healthy social circle. Ask yourself, do you feel they truly understand and accept you? Do you truly understand and accept them? Do you feel energized or energetically depleted after spending time with them? Do you include them in your life for the positive qualities they bring out in you, or not?

Chapter 3

Cooperating with your Ex to Dissolve the Marriage

" **W** hat?!? You're saying I am supposed to *cooperate* with my ex now?!?"

Yes.

If you want a divorce that is easier, less painful and more likely to set you and your family up positively for the future, you *must* understand that your marriage was a partnership. If you cooperatively dissolve the financial aspects of your marriage partnership, you will pave the way for becoming "parent partners" which we will talk about in Chapter 8. You actually need to team up and cooperate with the person you are divorcing to get the divorce itself right. It's an odd twist of fate, isn't it? You now need to form a decent working relationship with the person who is leaving you or whom you are leaving. It's not easy. But if you remain open and willing to dissolve the marriage partnership cooperatively, not only will the outcomes of your divorce be more thoughtful and mutually beneficial, you'll find that releasing your old life and creating a solid future will come more naturally and quickly.

If you have children or ongoing financial business together, a cooperative dissolution of the marriage partnership will benefit you for many years. Even if you don't have children or ongoing financial businesses together, a cooperative dissolution of the marriage partnership will benefit you emotionally. Whether long-term or short-term, the quality of the dissolution of the marriage partnership now will have significant impacts on your life going forward. No matter how resistant you feel to this idea — "Are you kidding me?!? I have to work cooperatively with *him/her*?!?" — trust me. The effort it takes will be well worth it in the long run.

And the truth is, it is hard to get to that level of cooperation by yourselves, but knowledgeable professionals can help get you there, as these two stories illustrate.

How Much?!?

Lisa and Donald, a couple in their early forties with no children, had tried to be cooperative with one another as I led them through discussions of dividing up the assets—but they often got stuck. Part of this was due to their natural competitiveness but a large part was from the advice of well-meaning (and unknowledgeable) friends. We were in the final stretch when Lisa put her foot down based on advice from a real estate buddy. "Donald took it upon himself to refinance the house, so he should be the one to cover all the fees for the new loan." "I took it out for both of us," Donald argued. "I shouldn't be stuck with them." They argued for several minutes before I interrupted, asking, "Do either of you know how much money you're arguing about?" They both shook their heads and I pointed out that the fees for the new loan on the refinance were minimal if they split it evenly. Lisa was sheepish when she realized she was arguing about such a small amount and was willing to compromise. Lisa and Donald also realized that they had so much pain and history from ending their relationship that the issue was not the loan fees but their own emotional fears and frustrations. By using a knowledgeable, professional mediator, they were more easily able to work together cooperatively.

How Dare You!?!

In another case, my clients Joanne and Mitchell were also feeling fearful from the breakup of their marriage, especially about finances. Mitchell had moved out of the house and needed finances to set up a new house. Joanne had stayed in the family residence with the two children and all of the household furnishings.

Mitchell and Joanne arrived for a mediation session and Joanne immediately expressed her anger at Mitchell for not being fair about the finances. Apparently Mitchell had deposited his $9,000 paycheck into the joint account and had immediately withdrawn $6,000. Mitchell was stunned that Joanne was upset by this. He thought it was reasonable because he was facing the expense of setting up a new household for himself. "Besides," he said, "we have over $40,000 in savings that Joanne is welcome to draw from if she needs it." Once Joanne and Mitchell were able to discuss this issue with me as their mediator in a neutral setting, Joanne was able to calm down and see Mitchell's actions from his point of view. Joanne and Mitchell both realized from this experience that building trust and cooperation were important for their future and moving forward.

In the stories above, you can imagine how differently it might have turned out without the willingness to work together cooperatively. Like those couples, your divorce will go much more smoothly if you are willing to work with your ex-spouse, learn to resolve conflict, and improve your communication skills. All of this will be easier if you remember you are making this effort for everyone— most of all yourself. The initial weeks and months in any divorce are challenging. To transition from being intimate marriage partners to dissolving the marriage partnership cooperatively is tricky. In this chapter, we'll discuss how to make that transition easier.

Old Dynamics

During a marriage, couples learn to relate to one another and create their own particular relationship dynamic for the marriage.

These dynamics can be blatant or subtle, positive or negative. We often just slip into a pattern of relating to one another without being aware of it. After several years, these patterns and dynamics become automatic, like a knee-jerk reaction. I would say that one of the main reasons couples divorce is that the patterns and dynamics they have developed are not healthy. Couples with healthy dynamics have a greater chance of working through difficulties and conflicts constructively together. Couples with unhealthy dynamics often haven't developed the skills necessary to face life's challenges together.

There is a good chance that the relationship dynamics that you and your soon-to-be ex have developed are not healthy. If that is the case, this is your opportunity to recognize what works and does not work about your patterns and make some changes. Both of you played a part in creating the dynamics of your marriage relationship. It only takes one person to shift the dynamic and create different ways of relating and communicating.

How do you identify the relationship dynamics of your marriage? Think about specific times when the two of you made a decision or faced a problem together. Were you each collaborative or combative? How well did you listen to one another? Did you reach a conclusion that was mutually acceptable? Did one of you consistently have the final say? What was your role in the interaction? Passive? Aggressive? Try to examine these questions without assigning "blame" (which we will discuss in more depth) by merely noticing what the patterns seem to be. How well did these patterns work for you?

The next step to improving your relationship dynamics is to focus on what *you* can change, *not* on what you think your spouse should change. You cannot change someone else; you can only change yourself. If you decide to no longer participate in the same way or participate in a different, more positive way, the relationship dynamic will change. This change may be subtle in the relationship at the start, but by staying the course with your own changed actions and reactions, you will see a greater change fairly quickly.

Respond Versus React

When we get stuck in a relationship dynamic or pattern, we tend to be *reactive* rather than *responsive*. *Reacting* is that knee-jerk feeling where you end up saying or doing something impulsively, almost as if you have no control. Know the feeling? It is when your emotions are triggered and those emotions determine your next move. It's when someone pushes your buttons—and who knows how to do that more effectively than your spouse? When we are *reactive*, we are falling victim to life, circumstances, other people and our own emotions. We speak and act out of fear, anger, or sadness. When we are operating from a reactive mode, we rarely make choices or decisions that are in anyone's best interest, especially our own. In reactive mode, we give up our power to choose wisely.

Responding on the other hand is calmer, more thoughtful and definitely more likely to get you where you want to be. This distinction between being *reactive* and *proactively responsive* can be confusing for some people. In his book, *7 Habits of Highly Effective People*, author Stephen Covey does a good job of explaining the difference. (If you haven't read this book, I highly recommend it. I re-read it often, and frequently suggest that my clients read it.)

Stephen's first habit in the book is: Be Proactive. By this he means to take initiative in life by realizing that your *decisions* determine the quality of your life, not your circumstances. He urges us to take responsibility for our choices and the consequences that follow. He writes, "Proactive people recognize that they are response-able." In other words, they do not simply react to someone else's words or actions or even their own emotions. They choose from a place of being responsible.

To be proactive rather than reactive, you need to learn to recognize when you are triggered, to listen to yourself in that moment, and to pause before you respond. That moment between the stimulus (when someone has pushed your buttons) and your response is your greatest place of power. In that moment, you have the freedom to choose how you will respond. Stephen Covey says this about it:

"One of the most important things you choose is what you say. Your language is a good indicator of how you see yourself. A proactive person uses proactive language—I can, I will, I prefer, et cetera. A reactive person uses reactive language—I can't, I have to, if only. Reactive people believe they are not responsible for what they say and do—they have no choice. Instead of reacting to or worrying about conditions over which they have little or no control, proactive people focus their time and energy on things they can control."

From this response-able place, let us talk about a main factor that prevents it: blame.

The Blame Game

One of the keys to becoming responsible and response-able is to stop the blame game. I touch on blame throughout this book because it is so prevalent in many divorces. Something—or most often, some*one*—must be to blame for the breakdown of the marriage! Countless hours are wasted trying to assign blame and that practice keeps us stuck in the emotions of guilt, anger, and/or sadness.

I know, sometimes it is very hard not to assign blame. Sometimes our sense of justice screams out, "This is just wrong." We want to blame the people who hurt us over and over again. Sometimes these people know that their actions are "wrong" by society standards, but they do them anyway, without compassion or empathy. Sometimes they know their behavior is wrong, and it bothers and shames them to do it—but they claim they can't help themselves. And sometimes they will claim their actions are justified. Nevertheless, the truth of the matter is, no matter what the circumstances, blame will not help you move forward.

Blame can be a habit that is an integral part of a relationship dynamic. It becomes a pervasive cycle of "he blames her then she blames him" or vice versa. It is contagious and research shows that blame is actually a form of self-defense to protect our own self-image. If we can blame someone else for our problems, then we do not have to point the finger at ourselves. If your ex-spouse blamed you for his or her own failures, you are likely to blame him/her for yours. It is a vicious cycle and to break the cycle can be a challenge.

When you blame another, in many ways you are denying your own power. If someone else's actions can "cause" you to act, think or feel a certain way, they control your destiny, don't they? Another's actions might create a particular circumstance, but what you do about that circumstance is totally up to you. What someone else says or does may "trigger" a reaction in you, but whether you act on that reaction is your choice—though in the heat of battle, it may not feel like it!

To lessen the reaction and take back some of your lost power, refrain from indulging in the blame game. Whether you're telling your story to yourself or others, avoid painting your ex-spouse as the bad person. Simply stick with the facts of "she did this" or "he said that." Pay close attention to what *you* did or said in reaction. Though it might have felt righteously delicious in the moment, did your *reaction* serve you in the long run? Are you proud of it? Would you have liked someone to react to you in that same way? Was there a better way to *respond?*

By the way, blaming yourself is no healthier than blaming your spouse. It is one thing to take responsibility for your part in the breakdown of the relationship. It is another thing to blame your-self as if your spouse was a victim of your actions. If you have done something within the relationship that you don't like, acknowl-edge it, apologize and make amends if you can, then move on. Use whatever regret you feel as a lesson learned. Holding on to guilt will only cloud your judgment and ability to respond proactively. It will *not* in any way help your spouse to heal and regain a sense of self-worth.

Recapturing Self-Esteem

Both parties in a divorce, but especially the person who did not choose to end the relationship, take a hit to their self-esteem.

Many people report feeling unlovable or unworthy as their marriage falls apart. In my experience, it is the rare individual who goes through a divorce without at least a few moments of wondering why they were not good enough, smart enough, mature enough, whatever enough to make the marriage work. Though you might learn something useful through this line of questioning, it is counter-productive to stay there. When your self-esteem is battered and bruised, you tend to feel defensive which kicks you back into *reactive* mode rather than response-able mode.

So now is the time to recover your self-esteem. You may need to push yourself a bit but there are a number of things that will help you feel better about yourself again. Some form of exercise can be really beneficial right now. Studies consistently find that regular exercisers are healthier, happier, and more productive than they were before they started exercising. Doing fun activities and hobbies you enjoy can be a real boost, as can giving back to the community through some form of volunteering. Surrounding yourself with people who are positive and believe in you is another way to shore up your self-confidence.

This solid sense of self-worth will also help break the cycle of the blame game. When you feel confident, you are in position to *respond* calmly and tactfully if your spouse still tries to blame you for what has happened. You will be able to acknowledge your part in the breakdown of your marriage and learn from it rather than becoming defensive. You will be able to stay above the fray of blame by keeping your self-esteem in good form.

And if these suggestions don't work for you, find a professional and talk it out. If you are feeling overwhelmed and still *reactive* about your relationship and the issues you need to resolve, seek out a divorce coach or other mental-health professional who can see the situation from a distance. Talking things over with a supportive professional may help to alleviate defensive reactions and help you find a foundation where you can be more responsive.

The Magic Key: Forgiveness

I can't emphasize enough the importance—and magic—of forgiveness during this process. At this point, forgiving your former spouse or yourself may still seem impossible. But keep in mind that forgiveness is not something you do for the person who has hurt you. It is something you do for yourself and for your children. As radio host Bernard Meltzer says, "When you forgive, you in no way change the past—but you sure do change the future."

Forgiveness is not about condoning or even completely forgetting harmful actions or words. It is about lightening your emotional burden. If you have children, this release will help you be a better parent and co-parent. Buddhists compare un-forgiveness to clutching a hot ember; hanging onto it doesn't harm the ember—only the one who won't let it go. Author, speaker Dr. Steve Maraboli says, "The truth is, unless you let go, unless you forgive yourself, unless you forgive the situation, unless you realize that the situation is over, you cannot move forward." And moving forward is what you want, right?

Much has been written about forgiveness and there are many processes to help you forgive yourself or others. The following is from Fred Luskin, PhD, director of the Stanford University Forgiveness Project and the co-chair of the Garden of Forgiveness Project at Ground Zero in Manhattan. He shares the following advice for forgiving another person.

1. **Find Your Voice:** Spend some time to know exactly how you feel about what happened. Get to the place where you can articulate what about the situation is not okay. Then tell a couple of trusted people about your experience, your thoughts and feelings.

2. **Do It for You:** Think of your un-forgiveness as hanging onto a hot ember. Don't do it to yourself. Make a commitment to do what you have to do to forgive because you will feel better. Forgiveness is for *you* and not for anyone else.

3. **Find Peace:** Forgiveness does not necessarily mean that you reconcile with the person who hurt you, and it certainly doesn't mean that you condone their actions. What you are after is peace. Forgiveness is the peace and understanding that come with releasing blame, taking the life experience less personally, and changing your internal story about the grievances.

4. **Put the Past in the Past:** Get a different perspective on your un-forgiveness. Recognize that your distress is coming from the hurt feelings, thoughts and physical upset you are suffering *now*, not whatever offended you or hurt you two minutes (or ten years!) ago. Forgiveness heals current hurt feelings and moves the past incident back where it belongs—in the past.

5. **Breathe:** In the instant you feel upset, take a deep breath. Then take another. Deep breathing is a simple stress-management technique which soothes your body's flight-or-fight response. It is the only thing you can do consciously to signal your unconscious physical responses to relax.

6. **Drop Expectations:** Let go of expecting things from other people that they do not choose to give you. Release the expectation that life has to hand you exactly what you want. Recognize the "unenforceable rules" you have about how life should be or how other people should behave. Remind yourself that you can move toward health, love, peace and prosperity by your own actions and choices.

7. **Face Forward:** Concentrate your energy into looking for ways to get your needs and goals met rather than focusing on the experience that hurt you. Instead of mentally replaying your disappointment in what *did not* work out for you, seek out new ways to get what you want.

8. **Get Even by Getting Better:** Remember that a life well lived is your best revenge. Instead of focusing on your wounded feelings—thereby giving power to the person who caused you pain—learn to look for and expand the love, beauty

and kindness around you. Forgiveness is about personal power.

9. **Tell It Differently:** Amend your grievance story. Start leaving out the parts about the hurt and emphasize the parts about the learning. Make it a hero's journey where you, the hero, found the courage to forgive.

The practice of forgiveness reduces hurt, anger, depression, and stress. It leads to greater feelings of hope, peace, compassion and self-confidence. Practicing forgiveness leads to healthy relationships as well as physical health. It also opens the heart to kindness, beauty, and love. So which will you choose?

For more information on forgiveness from Fred Luskin, visit the website www.learningtoforgive.com.

Your Choice

Divorce is a painful experience for everyone involved, but it is also an opportunity for change. If you can learn to work with your former spouse—despite your differences—you will have taken the first step toward building a rewarding new life. Your divorce can be a time when you learn to take total responsibility for your choices, actions and results. It is an opportunity to become proactive in being responsible for you. During this divorce process you will have the opportunity to choose contentment and responsibility or sadness, anger and blame. You have the choice of moving forward stronger or remaining wounded. You can choose courage or choose fear.

Every moment, every situation, every encounter during your divorce process provides a new choice. Every step gives you a perfect opportunity to do things differently and to produce new, more positive results. The greatest power you have is to take responsibility for responding, rather than reacting, to create an effective collaborative working relationship to dissolve your marriage partnership.

Chapter 4

Taking Charge of Emotions

In this School of Life, most of us experience a relationship breakup as one of our greatest challenges and lessons. Even if we do not consider ourselves "emotional," the breakdown of a marriage can activate a whole hoard of painful, confusing, sometimes out-of-control emotions. Operating out of highly intense emotions renders it difficult, if not impossible, to make important decisions.

For many of us, it takes a significant period of time to fully process all of these emotions so that we feel "complete" with what has happened. As with any life crisis, most healthy adults will eventually come to new understandings, releasing or lessening painful emotions to move on in life. But, until we let go of some of those emotions, they can toss us around, pushing us to say and do things we will regret later when we are more calm, cool and collected.

The problem is that the divorce process, with all of its decisions and choices and negotiations, more often than not happens *before* these emotions can be fully processed.

When negative emotions overwhelm you, it makes it difficult to see possibilities and solutions. Negative emotions push people to become entrenched in their positions, gridlocked by senseless power struggles. Such power struggles make it difficult to negotiate with positive results. If they do not take charge of these powerful emotions, even couples who could dissolve their marriages amicably end up in a court of law, handing over critical decisions to a judge (who has little time to completely understand their case due to over-scheduling in the courts) and two attorneys (who have been trained to be one-sided and adversarial). The process is not pretty, but divorcing spouses turn their cases and decisions over to the courts every day because they are polarized by negative emotions.

If you and your spouse can take charge of your negative emotions, even before you have fully processed them, you have the opportunity to make these important decisions for yourselves. Family law judges work hard to be fair, but they are not familiar with the two of you and what would best serve you. The people who know your circumstances best are you and your spouse. Keeping the decision-making process between the two of you with the help of qualified professionals will ensure your best interests are considered—but only if you take charge of your negative emotions during the process. If you do not, your negative emotions will force your divorce into the arms of adversaries and a family court judge.

To help you experience what I mean, think of someone you love who brings you an inner smile. Maybe it is the friend who always stands by you or that hairdresser who makes you laugh, or that creative cousin who has such an upbeat attitude. Maybe it is your grandmother because she always sees the best in you. As you think about him or her, notice how you feel emotionally and physically. I am guessing you feel something like joy, safety, peacefulness, and a flowing sense of connection to yourself and to this person. In this state of emotion, you are more kind, loving, and creative, as well as more open to possibilities and opportunities, right?

Now, think of someone who makes you feel afraid or angry. Really focus on whatever negative emotion you feel when thinking about this person. How does that make you feel emotionally and physically? Chances are you feel tense, shut down, constricted and less open. And rather than seeing possibilities and opportunities, you are probably only seeing potential threats and dangers. This state of emotion not only affects our health, it also keeps us from being our full, healthy potential as creative and productive people and parents. This is *not* the state that helps you make good choices or decisions.

So exactly how do you "take charge" of your emotions surrounding the divorce before they are fully processed?

Most of us know that simply "stuffing" our emotions is no good. Keeping a stiff-upper lip or clenching our teeth to keep emotions hidden is counter-productive. It requires tremendous energy and effort, and leaves us exhausted and tense—not a good frame of mind for solving problems, making decisions or resolving any kind of issue. And though we may not outwardly express our distress or anger, internally these emotions can still run the show, persuading us to make decisions that are *not* in our best interest.

So if neither allowing emotions to run wild or struggling to keep them bound and tied works, what do we do?

In my experience, our best results are created when we work *with* these emotions. We do not allow them to call the shots, but we don't deny them either. We gain mastery over them, while allowing the natural process of healing to continue.

Understanding Emotions

What are emotions? How do they work? Emotions are both biological and cognitive experiences. An emotion includes thoughts, bodily symptoms, motivation to respond or act, and expressions. Especially when you feel highly emotional, your thoughts stimulate a physical response and a strong desire to take action. For example, if you feel the emotion of fear, you may *think* you are in danger, your *body* (via an adrenaline rush) may feel jumpy or anxious and your immediate *reaction* may be to fight, freeze or flee.[1]

Although strong emotions can be problematic, they are also highly valuable. Emotions prompt and organize us for action. They provide us important information and trigger our instinctual and intuitive abilities. Emotions motivate us to move forward. Emotions help us communicate effectively with others and they can help us adapt to conditions.

As we have all experienced, emotions ebb and flow and do not last forever (although some last longer than others). The intensity of emotions varies from person to person, and varies within each of us from one situation to another. When you are in the middle of an emotional storm (which is often the case during the breakup of a marriage), it is important —and difficult—to remember that the emotions will flow in and out and will *not* last forever. Keeping in mind that the heightened emotions of today will one day be a vague memory can help you avoid reacting in the heat of the moment. As many a philosopher has said, "This too shall pass."

To prove this to yourself, think about a time in the distant past when you were ferociously angry with someone. Remember back and rate the heat of the emotion at that time based on a scale of 1 to 10. Did you say or do anything in the heat of anger? If so, how did that work out for you? How long did it take you to cool down? Once you cooled down, what was the level of intensity of your anger, from 1 to 10? And when you think about that incident today, how would you rate the emotion you currently feel about it?

Now think of a time of deep sadness in the past. At that time, how would you rate your level of sadness from 1 to 10? How long did it take you to feel better? When you think of that time today, how would you rate your sadness about it?

---

[1] Some of the best work on emotions has been done in Dialectical Behavior Therapy (DBT). Originally founded by Marsha Linehan, an American Psychologist, author and professor of psychology, DBT combines standard cognitive behavioral techniques for emotion regulation, reality testing concepts, acceptance and mindful awareness.

Next remember a fearful event in your past. On a scale of 1 to 10, how frightened would you say you were at the time? Do you remember your thoughts about the situation while you were in the very midst of your fear? Your reactions or actions to the fear you felt? How long did it take for you to become less fearful? When you relaxed, what was the strength of your fear on a scale of 1-10?

Taking this look back, you probably saw two things: (1) The intensity you felt at one time is no longer with you, and (2) the way you acted and things you said during the height of these emotions probably are not the choices you would make in a calmer state. As you move through this divorce, you will likely feel a tremendous amount of emotion, as well as its ebb and flow. Throughout the divorce process, you will benefit greatly if you allow the intensity of your emotions to subside before you take action on any major decision that needs to be made.

Major Emotions of Divorce

Divorcing couples usually run through the whole gamut of human emotions. In my experience, there are three emotions that are common to most of us in this situation: fear, anger, and sadness or depression. And if these specific emotions are not addressed, they can wreak havoc with the divorce process, causing much more misery than necessary. It is worthwhile to take a deeper look into these three. Odds are that you and your spouse are experiencing them.

About Fear

Divorce generates fear on a number of levels. The foundation upon which you have been living is breaking up and you are heading into unknown territory. Even if you were dissatisfied or unhappy in your marriage, the known still feels safer than that great unknown. We tend to project the "worst that can happen" in this unknown, exaggerating how bad things are or will be, which makes us unable to think clearly.

When we are living in fear, we tend to act out with anger, abuse, guilt, competition, and defensiveness. We feel insecure and that we are "lacking" in many ways. Left unchecked, fear can even lead to physical pain and illness. To make matters worse, fear breeds fear. The more we act out the emotion, the more fearful we become. By focusing on fearful thoughts, we sometimes attract that which we dread.

To shift from this place and break the chain of fear, we need to understand what we feel and acknowledge it. How do you know whether you are operating from fear? Take the following quiz.

- Do you feel you want to get revenge?

- Do you feel the need to defend yourself?

- Do you feel anxious in general or about specific issues?

- Do you feel you have been victimized?

- Do you feel paralyzed and unable to make decisions?

Mindfulness (as discussed in Chapter 2) can replace fear. In mindfulness, we are comfortable listening to all points of view. Mindfulness keeps us in the present without projecting into the future. In a mindful state, we do not make up our minds in advance about how things should be. We learn to stop believing there is only one way to do things.

Ask yourself the following questions to gauge your level of mindfulness:

- Are you able to focus on the here and now?

- Are you feeling a sense of emotional balance?

- Do you feel open to new ideas?

- Can you let go of knowing exactly what the outcome is going to be?

- Can you focus on the benefits for *everyone*, not solely on what *you* want?

About Anger

Anger is another primary emotion felt during divorce. In a sense, it is the flip side of fear. Anger during divorce is often due to a feeling that you are out of control, the feeling that you no longer have control of your life, your possessions or your future. Anger can also stem from a sense of betrayal, that vows were broken or trust shattered. Anger is a natural response. But it is a problem if it starts controlling you, your actions or your decisions.

We see a great deal of what we call "situational domestic violence" during divorce. In these cases, there has not been a history of domestic violence, but due to the situation of the breakup, one party or both cannot manage their anger or emotions. Because of this, Family Courts will order many divorcing spouses into anger management classes. If you feel that your own anger is taking control, try using the following tools:

1. **Look for warning signs**. When we become angry, our bodies exhibit signs such as a tight chest, a racing mind, shortness of breath, sweaty palms or getting flush. Learn to recognize these signs so you can intervene before you blow up.

2. **Take a time-out.** Ask for a break from the conflict. Tell the other person you feel you need a break to manage your anger so you do not hurt yourself or anyone else. Walk away from the situation until you feel calmer.

3. **Slow down your thoughts.** Count to ten. Before reacting to a tense situation, take a few moments to breathe deeply and count to 10. Slowing down can help defuse your temper.

4. **Ease up on the reins**. A false sense of urgency stems from a sense of self-importance and a need to control. Recognize that you do not need to control everything and always be in charge.

5. **Recognize your anger is a problem.** By recognizing that your anger has become a problem, you can ask for help.

Learn from others about how to stop yourself and find other ways to express yourself when you feel angry.

6. **Get some exercise.** Physical activity stimulates brain chemicals that can leave you feeling happier and more relaxed. If you feel anger escalating, go for a walk or run, or spend some time doing your favorite physical activity.

7. **Identify solutions.** Instead of focusing on what made you angry, work on resolving the issues or feelings of being out of control. Remind yourself that anger will not solve anything. You can find more creative and meaningful ways to resolve conflict or the sources of your anger.

8. **Use humor to release tension.** Humor can be a wonderful diversion from heated emotions. Lightening up can diffuse the tension anger brings on. Just be careful not to use sarcasm as it could make the feelings worse.

9. **Practice relaxation skills.** Listen to calming music, learn to breathe more deeply, do yoga stretches, or repeat a calming affirmation or word. Write in a journal or go to an anger management class or meeting.

10. **Take care of yourself.** Make sure you are getting enough rest, eating well, and exercising. All of these contribute to your ability to handle your emotions.

11. **Ask for professional help.** Never be afraid to ask for help. You may save someone's life or your own. You will find plenty of support in the area of anger management. No one needs to feel alone when it comes to this issue.

About Depression

The emotional and physical loss of a relationship can bring on depression. In fact, depression is more likely during divorce or during a relationship breakup than at most other times. This is caused by both mental and physical changes.

Managing depression is critical at a time when so many decisions need to be made. If there are any thoughts of harming yourself or others, the depression needs to be managed through medical treatment. If the depression is mild, taking care of yourself through diet, exercise, and meditation will be helpful. Finding a support group can help as well. Search online for organizations that can refer you to professionals who can help with depression. If depression interferes with your daily functioning, it is of utmost importance to you and your children that you reach out and get help.

Counseling

Sometimes you cannot solve a problem on your own. You may need someone with special training and experience to help you manage emotions during this difficult time. In a later chapter in this book, I will give you some helpful hints on how to find a good therapist.

Emotional Mindfulness

As we discussed in Chapter 2, mindfulness is a practice that many describe as "being awake" and it allows you to be more intentional in your actions. Being more emotionally mindful includes being aware of the emotions you experience and how you choose to react to them.

As you practice it, mindfulness becomes a form of emotional regulation which connects your awareness to your reactions. Part of the practice of emotional mindfulness is learning how to name and describe your emotions. Research has shown that paying attention to and verbalizing our emotions allows us to regulate them more easily, to tone them down, or simply accept them.

For many of us, emotional mindfulness is not a familiar experience. Especially in Western cultures, we rarely pay attention to one thing at a time. We are watching TV while paying the bills while talking to our teenagers who are texting to their friends as they do their homework! And we spend most of our time distracted rather than focused or paying attention to emotions or even physical sensations. As British educator Sir Ken Robinson describes it, our Western school systems lead us to believe that our bodies are merely vehicles for taxiing our heads around!

So if the concept of emotional mindfulness feels foreign to you, join the club! But it is not something that is esoteric or complicated. It is really quite simple, though it does take time and practice to make mindfulness a part of your daily routine.

Start by observing and naming what you are feeling right this moment: your emotions and physical sensations. For now, hold your thoughts and judgments gently in the background as you turn your complete attention to merely observing what you feel. Just see what sensations and emotions are there without changing them. Notice if you react to the experience of your emotions, and allow that reaction to be gently in the background. Observe and notice how your emotions affect you. As thoughts and judgments pop up (and they will!), nudge them gently to the background and refocus on your sensations and emotions. Pay attention to the input from your five senses—sight, sound, touch, smell and taste. Be alert to what comes your way.

Next, describe to yourself the emotions you have observed. Be descriptive, but keep it simple and nonjudgmental. Notice that as you describe your emotions, you are more than those emotions; you are also the one who can observe them.

Choosing emotional mindfulness—rather than allowing your negative emotions to run your life—connects you to a more positive, intuitive, and nurturing side of yourself. When we operate from mindfulness, we open ourselves to more peace, creativity, kindness and a greater overall sense of wellbeing in our lives.

Disarming your Emotional Triggers

Emotional triggers are events *outside* of you or thoughts *inside* of you that activate certain emotions. Remember the emotions that came up instantly when you thought of someone you love or someone you fear? Your thought of that person was the trigger. Even simple, everyday occurrences can trigger strong emotions. Think of how you feel when you are in a hurry and get stuck in a long line at the supermarket or when you misplace your purse or wallet.

Some of the strongest triggers happen within relationships, especially relationships that have turned sour. Her questions may trigger a feeling of defensiveness. His silence may trigger the feeling of rejection. She sighs and you feel guilty. He raises his voice and you feel frightened. Even the way your spouse addresses you can set off a feeling of anger!

The issues that are discussed during the divorce process can also be triggers. For example, many people get emotional while talking about money or about the futures of their children. Your spouse may hit a nerve if he talks about leaving his current job, or you may feel emotional about certain assets and their disposition. Divorce is filled with emotional triggers that can set off feelings of fear, guilt, anger, or sadness. All of this is perfectly normal, but you want to stay in charge of those emotions so they do not cloud your judgment.

Identifying the things that trigger your negative emotions can help you deal with them when they surge strongly. Of course, it is especially helpful if you can be aware what buttons might get pushed *before* you have already reacted to them. To help identify your personal triggers, I recommend you maintain a journal about your day-to-day experiences during the divorce process. Pay particular attention to times when a strong negative emotion flooded in. What set it off? Backtrack until you can identify the moment that emotion started. Was it something that was said? Something someone did? An internal line of thinking? Write down what you discover, maybe even keeping a list of those specific things that trigger you. Once you have identified what triggers you, you can start working with it in several ways.

Rehearsal Exercise

First, you can rehearse prior to a situation that is likely to trigger you. Say, for instance, you will be meeting with your spouse to discuss finances, and you have identified that talking about money makes you feel panicky. Prior to the meeting, take a few moments to sit in a quiet space. Take a few deep breaths and imagine the meeting in your mind. Imagine yourself feeling totally calm and resourceful. If that seems difficult, take a few more deep breaths and try again. If you *did* feel calm and resourceful, how would that feel physically? What would your posture be like? How would you speak and listen? Get as much of that experience as you can.

Athletes use this visualization technique all the time to improve their performances. They imagine the ball landing softly on the green or how they feel soaring through the air off a ski jump. So rehearse yourself as being in the emotional state that you want to have. Whatever you do, do *not* rehearse yourself in your old panicked (or other negative emotion) mode! We often misuse the power of our imagination to rehearse everything we *don't* want to happen rather than what we want! That just helps us get better at being worse than we want to be.

Heat of Battle Exercise—Push Pause

Naturally, there will be times when you get caught off guard—life is full of surprises! You will get triggered and feel that rush of emotion before you know what is happening. When you do, stop. Push pause. Take a few deep breaths to calm yourself. Let the whole scene freeze if you need to. In most situations, just because it is your turn to say or do something, does not mean you have to! Keep breathing until you feel the emotion subside. If you still feel highly charged with emotion, you can even excuse yourself and take a brisk walk outside for a few moments. Or table the issue for another time entirely.

It may feel uncomfortable to push pause and remain silent. You may feel pressure to continue even though you know your emotions are at the boiling point. Stop. By taking the time to diffuse the trigger, the entire process will be much easier on you and produce better, more sustainable results in the long run.

Challenging Your Self-Talk

As we discussed, your thoughts can trigger emotions. Challenging and changing your thoughts is another way to work with emotional triggers.

When we leave a relationship and have a marriage breakup, we leave with our own assumptions about what went wrong. This creates a story that we tell ourselves, often over and over and over. We get more and more detailed about it: what our spouse did wrong, what we should have said at the time, what it *really* meant when he/she did or said whatever they did or said. The story gets blown up into full Technicolor including blame, criticism, judgment, and self-justification. And whether your particular story paints you or your spouse as the "bad guy," that story becomes a strong trigger for all of your negative feelings around the divorce.

The more often you tell the story and more you buy into it, the more inflexible and enmeshed in negativity you become. The story creates its own little conclusions: "My spouse is a jerk." Or "I am stupid." Or "I will never trust anyone again." Or "I am obviously not lovable." These little conclusions end up having big consequences. They become the "self-talk" that will guide your actions and decisions going forward. Learning to challenge this self-talk, and even the story that prompted it, is an important tool for taking charge of your emotions during the divorce process.

Inquiry Exercise—Challenging Your Story

One of the best ways to challenge the self-talk is to ask inquiring questions. Byron Katie[2] has done some wonderful work around examining self-talk through inquiry. Katie's goal is to help us break away from the stories that create negative self-talk and keep us limited and unhappy. Katie says that our stories are based on the *assumptions* we make about others and that it is important to question those assumptions. Byron Katie describes her work as a way of "identifying and questioning the thoughts that cause the

---

[2] Author, teacher Byron Katie can be found at: http://www.thework.com/index.php

anger, fear, depression, addiction, and violence we often feel." She teaches us to examine our assumptions by asking four questions. The questions seem simple, but if you take the time to answer them seriously, they can be quite profound and help you uproot negative thoughts and feelings that are holding you back. The four questions are:

1. Is it true?

2. Can you absolutely know that it's true?

3. How do you react, what happens, when you believe that thought?

4. Who would you be without the thought?

Apply the four questions to your own story about your divorce. It is most helpful if you ask it about each part of the story. When asking these four questions, you want to not only apply it to the *facts* of your story but especially to the underlying *assumptions* that you have around those facts. For example, part of the story may be that your spouse had an affair. She has admitted it so you know it is true. But the underlying *assumptions* you have attached to that fact might be things like, "So she never really loved me" or "So, I can't trust her about anything ever" or "I must have done something wrong that she would do such a thing." Make sure that you ask the four questions about *all* parts of your story.

Seeing It Differently Exercise

Another helpful way to change your story and the negative self-talk it creates is to ask yourself the question: How could I see this differently? In this practice, without necessarily questioning whether your story and assumptions are true or not, you let yourself take on a different perspective.

Haven't you noticed that people can live through the exact same experience yet tell a totally different story about it? For instance, you may have grown up at the same time in the same household with three siblings. More often than not, the four of you will be different and unique in the adults you have become. When you get together to reminisce about your childhood, odds are that your stories about those times will be different. One sibling will recall an uncle as mean and patronizing while another sibling will recall him as funny and entertaining. You might remember family holidays as warm and loving while your brother thought they were boring or stressful.

We all process information through our filters, but through this question you have the opportunity to try on other filters. "How could I see this differently?" Let yourself come up with a totally different story—especially different assumptions about *why* anything happened. Does this new story make you feel differently? Is it possible that there is some truth in this new story? Maybe there is a new perspective that gives you food for thought and calms down the negativity that your old story created?

The point of all of these exercises is to help you experience the control you have over your emotions, even those emotions that seem to tie you in knots and overwhelm you at times. Part of making your divorce process as easy and beneficial as possible is to take charge of your emotions and to get you in the state of mind to produce positive outcomes for you and your family. It does take a little work but you will find that the rewards are worth it.

Chapter 5

Build Your Foundation of Well-Being

If you were planning to run a marathon, you would make sure that your body was in shape and that you were mentally prepared to make it all the way to the finish line, right? If you were about to facilitate a non-stop, week-long meeting where important decisions were to be made by a group of people with conflicting agendas, you would make sure that you were rested, mentally clear, and feeling calm and confident, right?

In many ways, to get the best possible outcomes, you want that type of personal preparation for your divorce.

Throughout the book, we have talked about specific challenges you will face during this process and how to deal with them. Over the years, I have also seen that couples who take care of themselves and their own general well-being are much more capable of moving through the issues and developing positive solutions than those who are generally stressed out and exhausted. Their foundation of general health and wellness served them well in handling the pressures, emotions and decisions of the divorce itself.

For example, Sam and Kathy were both emotionally and physically exhausted when they came to me for their divorce. Kathy was impatient, distracted, and snapped at me when I asked basic questions. She then apologized for her demeanor saying, "This is me at my absolute worst. I really am a nice person and generally easy to get along with. But lately I snap at the slightest thing." Kathy also said that she had been under so much stress and overwhelm about the breakup of the marriage that she had not been taking care of herself.

She was no longer doing her regular exercise routine or her yoga and meditation sessions. She had also started binging on sugar, her emotional "comfort food."

Sam admitted that he was not thinking clearly either and had not slept well since the two of them had decided to end the marriage. To distract himself from his distress, he had gotten into the habit of watching late-night TV which meant he only slept for three or four hours each night. The lack of sleep was affecting him at work and Sam's boss had even given him a warning about his performance.

I told Kathy and Sam that I understood this was a very difficult and traumatic time in their lives. But for the sake of their children and themselves, a foundation of well-being was critical to being able to work through the decisions they needed to make. I commended both of them for recognizing that they needed to get back on track. In that session, Sam committed to focusing on his need for sleep and said he would go back to reading in the evening, a great sedative for putting him to sleep. Kathy was eager to get back to her regular exercise and stress reduction routine, and vowed to shake the sugar habit.

About six weeks later, Sam and Kathy came for their second session. I hardly recognized the two of them! Kathy was cooperative, level-headed and attentive to the process. Sam looked rested and was more alert. I commented on how well they both looked. Kathy explained that, after our last session, she was able to see how the lack of taking care of herself was really causing more than just physical and emotional harm. It was also going to negatively impact some of the most important decisions she needed to make in the divorcing process.

If you do not have a foundation of wellness, it is important you make it a priority now. This chapter presents ways you can support that foundation. Many of my clients have benefitted from these recommendations, and I believe maintaining your own personal wellness at the time of divorce can be as important as anything else you do to cope with the stress. If you are tempted to skip over this chapter, please don't!

Get Moving

Exercise and movement will not only help you feel good and think more clearly, it also has a side benefit of helping you look good too. And who doesn't feel more confident and happy when they are looking good? When we talk about "exercise," we often think of it as another burdensome task on our to-do list. Even in normal times, it can feel like a stretch (okay, pun intended!) to spend time at the gym. And most people going through a divorce already feel maxed out time-wise and energy-wise with all of the changes and issues they are dealing with.

But I would like you to look at exercise in a new way. I'd like you to think of it as something that is easy, natural and pleasurable. Think of it as "movement" and just a way of life. When we experience conflict or stress, we often hold tension in our bodies. Vigorous movement releases endorphins, the natural chemical in our brains that make us feel good. But almost any kind of movement will help you move out of stress and into a more positive state of mind.

Start with simple ways you can incorporate movement into what you already do. For example, when you get up in the morning, take a few minutes to wake up your body by stretching. You do not have to attend a yoga class to do yoga stretches. Just hit the floor and stretch as you roll out of bed. You can stretch your back gently as you put on your socks. You can stretch your calf muscles as you brush your teeth or consciously stretch your shoulders as you reach into that high cupboard for the cereal.

Think of parking the car in a new way when you run errands. Look for a parking spot that is a distance from the store so you get the benefit of extra walking. Better yet, walk or ride your bike to stores that are close by. Take the long route through the grocery store, maybe heading down aisles you usually skip. Enter the department store through the entrance that is farthest away from your destination.

At work, climb the stairs rather than taking the elevator. Walk over to your colleague's office rather than calling or sending an email. Get out and walk for a few minutes during your lunch hour. If you spend much of the day in front of your computer, stand up and stretch every 30 minutes. (One of my clients even sets an alarm on her laptop to remind her to do this.) Walk around, or at least stand up, while you are on conference calls.

At home, turn off the television, turn on the music and move. Boogie around the living room with your kids, your dog or just yourself. Listening to music you love naturally increases your desire for movement. Even just listening to music has beneficial effects on the brain, but adding movement is even better. Sing out loud, even if only in the shower or in your car. Singing frees negative emotions, gets you breathing more deeply, and helps you feel energized.

Make movement a family affair. Rather than sitting at home, get outside with your children. Take a walk, go to the park, drive to some place beautiful for a short hike. Explore your city with your children by going to local museums or tourist attractions. Or join a gym. It is a great place for families and most gyms and health clubs have programs for children too. Whatever you choose to do, get out and get moving together!

Use your leisure time differently. Rather than watching sports events, find a sport that you enjoy doing yourself. The possibilities are endless: bicycling, hiking, swimming, golfing, bowling, walking, rollerblading, skiing, or tennis. It might be a sport you did as a kid or one you have never tried, but do not be afraid to experiment.

One of my clients took up tennis the year she and her ex separated. She was amazed at how much negative emotional energy she could release on the tennis court. Little things that used to upset her in the early months of the separation hardly got to her at all once she got involved in the running, serving, reaching, and swinging movements of tennis. Before taking up tennis, she had felt overwhelmed by the negative emotions and the smallest of things drove her crazy. But by doing a sport she loved, she became much more calm and grounded.

Everyone can incorporate movement into their lives. Find types of movement that fit your body and lifestyle—and notice the positive change in your emotions and mental clarity!

Eat Well to Be Well

"You are what you eat." Most of us know what we should eat but we do not always do it. Foods that are not good for us are often convenient and give us temporary comfort. Foods that are healthy often take a little more preparation and forethought. We need motivation. Right now, your motivation for eating healthy food is your own well-being. Eating well will help you have the energy you need as a newly single person. It is also a great opportunity to be a good role model for your children.

In *You on a Diet*, Dr. Mehmet Oz writes, "Eating right shouldn't be about feeling bad. It should be about feeling strong, increasing energy, living better, feeling healthier, and having more fun than a front-row rock fan." I am a big fan of Dr. Oz. If you have a DVR or recorder or are home during the day, try watching his daily program. He gives great advice for healthy eating with examples and research that are highly motivating![1] The *You* books (*You on a Diet, You Staying Young*, et cetera) by Dr. Oz and Dr. Roizen are easy

---

[1] Take a look at his website: www.DoctorOz.com

to read and can help you understand your biology and deal with physical challenges you face.

Mood Food

In addition to affecting your physical health, food can directly affect your moods and emotions. Have you ever noticed that a meal heavy in carbohydrates like pasta or breads can leave you feeling groggy and tired? How about that sugar high and subsequent crash from candy or desserts made with refined sugar?

Elaine Magee, MPH, RD is the nutrition expert on WebMD. In a recent article, she reviewed the research about foods that affect your emotions both positively and negatively.[2] Some of her conclusions are:

1. Do not Banish Carbs—Just Choose Smart Ones: Surprisingly, diets that are extremely low in carbohydrates increase fatigue and decrease motivation to exercise. To enhance your mood and energy levels, include "smart carbs" into your diet: legumes, whole grains, fruits and vegetables.

2. Get More Omega-3 Fatty Acids: Foods like fatty fish, walnuts and flaxseed may be beneficial in dealing with depression.

3. Eat a Good Breakfast: Didn't your mother always tell you to do that? Research shows that skipping breakfast leads to more fatigue and anxiety. (By the way, coffee with a Pop Tart does not qualify as a "good breakfast!")

4. Get Enough Vitamin D: Vitamin D increases serotonin (which helps regulate mood, sleep and appetite) in the brain. Research shows that Vitamin D can help people with depression.

---

[2] http://www.webmd.com/food-recipes/features/how-food-affects-your-moods

There is also plenty of research available now about how food affects the functioning of the brain. Dr. Daniel Amen, a psychiatrist and nationally recognized expert on the relationship between the brain and behavior, recommends a "brain healthy diet." This includes protein, such as turkey or chicken, whole grains, green leafy vegetables, and healthy fats that contain omega-three fatty acids, which are found in tuna, salmon, avocados, walnuts and other foods.

Dr. Amen writes, "Since the brain is 85% water, anything that dehydrates you is bad for the brain, such as alcohol, caffeine, excess salt or not drinking enough fluids." Dr. Amen urges patients to stop poisoning their brains: "Do not put toxic substances in your body. If you poison your brain you poison your mind."

The foods you eat have a direct correlation on how clearly you can think and how stable and positive you feel emotionally. Especially during the stress of your divorce process, you will benefit greatly from eating foods that support your physical, mental and emotional health. If you have specific health issues, talk to a licensed nutritionist or a doctor about changing your diet to enhance your well-being.

I learned the most about nutrition and wellbeing from the Optimum Health Institute (OHI) which offers a holistic healing program that promotes the well-being of your body, mind, and spirit. I first attended OHI about 15 years ago and return there each time I need a recharge or reminder of how to maintain my foundation of health. OHI is an inexpensive retreat center for wellness, providing classes on nutrition, proper food combinations, exercise, and stress release.[3]

---

[3] You can find more information about OHI on their website: www.optimumhealth.org

Chapter 6

It's All about Communication

Divorce can create a hostile environment. Learning to communicate your needs in this environment may be one of the toughest challenges you face, but you can help change the mood of this hostile environment by the way you communicate. During the marriage you most likely set up a communication style with your spouse and a specific way you communicated your needs. If the two of you had a respectful communication style, this chapter will help support that. If the communication style during your marriage was disrespectful (and therefore one of the reasons you are leaving the marriage) this chapter will be more challenging. However, with patience and by staying self-aware, you can change how you communicate your needs and how you are heard.

Listening to Understand

In Stephen Covey's *7 Habits for Highly Effective People,* Habit #5 is: Seek First to Understand, Then to Be Understood. Covey writes, "If you're like most people, you probably seek first to be understood; you want to get your point across. And in doing so, you may ignore the other person completely, pretend that you're listening, selectively hear only certain parts of the conversation or attentively focus on only the words being said, but *miss the meaning entirely.*"

Covey believes that this happens primarily because most of us listen with the intent of how we will reply; we are not listening to really understand the speaker's intent. Some of us are so busy coming up with what we want to say next, we hardly hear a word that is said, much less grasp the meaning of what someone is saying to us.

There is an old maxim that says, "You are given two ears and only one mouth for a reason." To relate successfully to others, most of us need to spend more time listening and less time speaking. We all want to be heard. But when we only half-listen to others and let our eyes glaze over as we prepare what we will say next, people recognize that they are not being heard. In response, they tune us out as well.

By not bringing our full attention to the task of listening, we miss opportunities to understand the other person and miss possibilities for creative problem-solving. It is hard to understand or come to resolution when you only absorb a small portion of the information you are being given.

We also hear through our own filters, those attitudes and assumptions we bring to every encounter. We hear what we *expect* to hear, not what someone has really said. Think about it: have you ever reacted in hurt or anger to a comment from someone? (Of course you have! We all have had that experience.) What meaning did you assign to that comment? What agendas or intentions did you assume the speaker held?

Now, if that same comment was made by someone else, such as a kind, trusted and loyal friend, would you react the same way? Probably not. The filters (assumptions and attitudes) you place on someone largely determine what you "hear" him or her saying and how you react. If you think someone is dishonest, a compliment can be heard as an attempt at manipulation. If you assume someone thinks you are not very smart, a small correction may feel like a slap in the face. By the same token, if you assume that someone thinks you are great, brilliant, handsome and sincere, every comment they make to you may feel terrific!

Within a close relationship, we build up a multitude of assumptions that can thwart effective listening. Because we have been intimate with our spouse, we assume (usually mistakenly!) that we understand where he or she is coming from, their motivations, intentions and desires. We assume that we know what he or she *really* thinks about us. We can cite history to "prove" our theories and assumptions, though the truth is that the history in our minds has been colored by our filters as well.

We can never totally get rid of these filters. But if we cling to them too tightly, it is difficult, if not impossible, to understand what someone else is truly saying. Covey calls this listening "autobiographically." To the best of your ability, you want to listen openly and attentively, with fresh ears as if you are hearing the other person speak for the first time. This is called "listening to understand." Difficult, yes. Impossible? No.

We have all had moments of autobiographical listening or focusing on what we want to say rather than what is being said to us. Check to see if any of these listening patterns apply to the way you listen to your spouse:

- Listening so you can gather ammunition for an attack. Focusing on hearing when your spouse slips up and says something wrong, unkind or untrue. That is the "gotcha!" method of listening. It is the type of listening that debaters—and attorneys!—are taught to use.

- Listening so your spouse is obligated to listen to you in return. In a sense, you are not really listening. You are just waiting for your turn. Your mouth is closed—but so are your ears! Usually in this pattern, you know what you want to say. You have scripted it out and maybe even rehearsed it. Rather than listening, you are just waiting for your opening.

- Listening to buy time so you can plan what to say next. You allow your spouse to yammer away while you concentrate on how to say what you want to say next. In this case, your mind is usually so busy crafting a response to a comment that was made earlier in the conversation that you have not heard a word since.

- Listening while feeling rattled by too much emotion. Most of us know that we should bring someone along if we are going to see the doctor about a serious illness. Why? Because when a doctor delivers bad news, we are usually too stunned and upset to hear anything she says next. If your spouse delivers some "bad news," you are probably not in condition to listen well.

If you can relate to any of the patterns above, you are not really listening to understand. It happens to all of us at times. To test to see if you *are* really listening, ask yourself: Could I repeat back what was just said to me? Could I ask meaningful questions about what was said? Do I feel that I really understand my spouse's perspective in what was said? If you are truly willing to listen to understand your spouse, communication during the divorce process will be much more productive and less stressful—and the results will be much more beneficial for both of you.

Here are some tips to enhance your listening-to-understand skills:

1. Practice when it is not important. Concentrate on listening when in casual conversation with friends or the check-out clerk at the grocery store. Notice any assumptions you have about the other person and let them go. Concentrate on what is being said as if you will be tested on it later!

2. Be curious and ask questions. Being curious does not mean you are agreeing with whatever is being said. You may even begin by saying, "I am curious about this. Tell me more, but please understand my curiosity does not mean I am in agreement. I just would like to understand with more

detail." Have the attitude that the other person can teach you something you have never known before.

3. Notice your own emotional state. If you are cranky, you will hear things in a different way than if you are feeling in love with the world! To listen well, bring yourself to a more neutral state. Breathe deeply to gather yourself. If you are too upset to calm yourself, table the discussion until you can do so.

4. Remember your mindfulness practices from Chapter 2. Mindfulness is that state of active, open attention. You observe what you are thinking and feeling without judging it as either good or bad. You observe whoever is with you from that same sense of attentiveness without judgment. (Yep. It takes practice!) Pay attention to body language, intonation and energy as well as the words themselves.

5. Listen to gather information. (And by this, I don't mean to gather ammunition!) When your spouse speaks, he is giving information about how he feels, what he wants, what is happening in his life. Or she may have factual information about family assets and obligations. Treat all of it as useful information that will help make your divorce process go more smoothly.

6. Hold your tongue! Avoid speaking without thinking. Allow silence to make sure that your spouse is completely finished. Allow silence so you have time to develop a thoughtful response.

7. Practice during shorter conversations. Many couples who divorce have ceased to really listen to one another long before the decision to separate occurs. Many have not had conversations beyond "What's for dinner?" for years! Meetings for divorce settlements often last one to two hours. If you are not proficient at listening to understand your spouse, two hours of listening can seem like an eternity! To develop your skills, practice this form of listening in shorter spurts. Take one small topic at a time, focusing on listening.

8. Try to empathize. This can be challenging! But try to empathize with your ex-spouse, without agreeing or being manipulated by them, so that they feel heard. I think of empathy as the understanding that "we are all doing the best we can at any point in time." We make mistakes. We do things we regret, but with rare exceptions, we are not intentionally evil or harmful.

9. Separate the person from the issue. Recognize that your spouse is probably not just being difficult. Most likely, they have real and valid reasons for thinking and feeling the way they do. Assume (until proven otherwise!) that they are sincere in what they say. Listen to the issue being addressed as neutrally as you can. If you separate the problem from the person, you will be able to hear what real issues need to be resolved.

Listening Affirmations

There is such incredible power in listening that I cannot emphasize enough how critical it is—and how much it will impact your divorce process. This is especially true during discussions that are highly charged with emotion or those when difficult decisions are to be made. Unfortunately, our ability to listen well often falls away during the very times when it is most important!

To help prepare for the crucial discussions, use the list of listening affirmations below. When you know you will be having a challenging conversation, pick one or two of these to help your listening. Jot your chosen listening affirmations on a 3x5 card. Review them right before you enter the discussion.

- I will consider whether either of us is upset and if we should have this discussion later instead of now.

- I accept that the other person may choose not to discuss this topic with me now.

- I will engage in our discussion cooperatively, as a collaborator.

- I will remember that the other person has the right to have different views and opinions than mine.

- I invite and encourage the other person's ideas.

- I listen to the other person without interrupting.

- I listen to the other person with the same respect I have for a good friend.

- I do not formulate rebuttals or clever come-backs while listening.

- I make an effort to truly understand what the person is trying to say.

- I make an effort to understand the other's feelings and perspective.

- I stick to the topic at hand.

- I focus on being interested and curious rather than judging, criticizing, or consoling.

- I will distinguish between whether the other person is asking for my opinion or simply sharing information.

- Before I offer my opinion, I ask whether the other person is interested in hearing it. If not, I wait until another time to express it.

- I notice my reactions during the discussion and put them to the side so I can listen.

Communicating Your Needs

Though most of us learn how to talk by the time we are toddlers, many of us are not taught to *communicate* well, a skill that is critical to ensuring a smooth and positive divorce process.

Communicating well does not just mean that you can state your case. To me, communicating well means you are able to clearly state your thoughts and feelings in a way that your listener can truly absorb. Your listener *cannot* absorb what you are communicating if your words and actions feel threatening. So a big part of good communication is helping your listener feel secure and as open as possible to what you have to say. Several components support this: good listening (listening to understand), clear intention, good non-verbal expression, tone of voice, and careful word choices.

Bottom Line: What is Your Intention?

A writer friend of mine coaches her friends on their written communications, including personal and business letters. She says that it always gets down to intention. She asks, "What do you really want from this communication? Do you want to lecture them, or preserve the relationship? Do you want to make them feel dimwitted, or do you want your money back?" Before you send that email or have that phone call, think about what you *truly* want at the end of the day.

What is your bottom-line intention during this divorce pro-cess? Do you want your spouse to feel horrible, or do you want to work out an equitable settlement and move on with your life? Do you want to make sure your spouse agrees that you are right and he/she is wrong (by the way, don't hold your breath on that one!), or do you want to know your best interests are considered as the two of you separate your lives? If you are looking for re-venge, you probably are not interested in communicating well. But if what you want is the most positive outcome possible from your separation, it is important to keep *that* intention foremost in your mind.

What do you want? What do you need? Now is the time to get clear on this. I am not talking about the "stuff," the material aspects of what you will get out of the divorce. This is about the *qualities* you want and need, such as respect, fairness, the sense that you have been heard and your opinions valued. List those qualities.

Next, ask yourself: Are those the same qualities I intend to offer my spouse throughout this process?

Non-Verbal Communication

In communication, it is said that 7% of what is communicated is in the words you say, 38% is in your tone of voice and 55% is in your body language! If you think about it, it makes sense. Imagine someone approaching you with a tense face and aggressive posture and asking, "What's up with you?" Now imagine that same person in a relaxed posture with a smile on his face. Wouldn't the same question feel very different to you? One would probably feel like a threat and the other like an invitation to share.

Now imagine someone squirming and looking down at his feet as he tells you, "I think I would be a good candidate for that job." Imagine that same person looking you confidently in the eye with a smile on his face. Who would you believe? Most of us tend to read these non-verbal clues similarly.

To communicate effectively, your physiology—facial expression, body posture, eye contact—should be relaxed, engaged and non-confrontational. This is actually quite natural to most of us when we are in comfortable or enjoyable situations. Having that same open physiology with your spouse during this time may take some effort, practice, and mindfulness. But with a little attention and practice, you will be surprised at how much easier your conversations with your spouse become, whether during divorce settlement meetings or just minor discussions. Here are some areas to pay attention to:

Before meeting with your spouse, take a moment to breathe deeply and relax your jaw, neck, and shoulders. Stand or sit comfortably in a posture that is neither too aggressive (chest puffed out, head pushed forward) nor too submissive (collapsed, head down). If you lean forward slightly, do so with a feeling of connecting, not overpowering. If you lean back slightly, do so feeling patient, not uninvolved. Face toward your spouse, not away. Turning away or to the side is a sign of cutting someone off. Your posture should signal your spouse that you are willing to work together.

Be aware of your gestures. Are they sharp and demanding? Fists clenched? Any hostility in your gestures will elicit defensiveness from your spouse. Are your hands nervous, anxious? Your spouse may read this as insincerity or lack of confidence. Are you prone to drumming or tapping your fingers? Often this is read as impatience. If you are a person who expresses with your hands, allow your gestures to be relaxed and open-handed. Often, it is easiest to keep your hands quiet and still.

When you meet with your spouse, maintain a consistent, non-invasive eye contact. Gently observe your spouse as she speaks. This will help her feel understood and respected. Also look your spouse in the eye when *you* speak to express confidence and sincerity in what you are saying. This also gives you the opportunity to gauge your spouse's reactions.

Allow your face to be as relaxed and neutral as possible but don't try to paste a phony cheerfulness on your face that you don't feel. A neutral face is attentive, interested, and non-judgmental. Your face will express this naturally the more you encourage yourself to actually feel that way! As your spouse speaks, nod encouragingly to show support, not necessarily agreement.

Tone

The tone of what you say reveals the intention behind what you say. Take the simple question, "Why do you want that?" You could ask that question with hostility, curiosity, suspicion, or compassion. That question could come from fearful place or an angry one. The tone with which the question is asked would determine your reactions to it, wouldn't it? Your questions and statements will all be interpreted through the tone you use.

What is the best tone of voice for effective communication? It is the tone that, like your body posture, expresses respect, willingness, and neutrality. In asking questions, your tone will be most effective if it is curious and interested, not accusatory or hostile to put your spouse on the defensive. In making statements about your desires or opinions, you will get the best response using a tone that is confident yet not argumentative or demanding.

To practice this, simply pay attention to yourself in your daily interactions with others. Notice how your tone sounds when you are with people you respect and admire. Notice how it changes around people you do not like or trust. Be aware of your tone when you are agreeing or collaborating with someone. Is it different when you are in disagreement, debating a point? The tone that will make your divorce process much easier is one that expresses respect and willingness to collaborate.

The Words You Speak

Words can heal and words can hurt. Those engaged in destructive conflict often use inflammatory words that make the conflict worse. In contrast, those engaged in *constructive* conflict choose their words wisely. Here are some tips to help with that:

1. **Slow it down**. To be able to *choose* your words, slow down your emotions and consider what you truly think, feel, want, and need in the moment. To slow down and give yourself time, begin with something like, "Thank you for meeting with me" or "I appreciate your willingness to talk about this subject." Slow down your speech. It takes someone else longer to understand and perceive the ideas you are sharing than it does for you to speak them.

2. **Ground yourself in the now**. Ground yourself in present-moment feelings; this moment and only this moment, letting go of past hurts or disappointments.

3. **Focus on Solutions.** Focus on solutions, not problems, to keep the door open for constructive resolution to take place. Leave the anger, accusation, and finger-pointing out of what you say.

4. **Allow silence.** Be aware of rambling to fill in space. Pause before responding or asking questions to let your spouse completely finish what he is saying.

5. **Own your own feelings**. You are responsible for how you feel, not your spouse. By this I mean, avoid using phrases like, "You *made me feel* like an idiot." Instead, to express how you feel, say, "When *you do X, I feel Y.*"

6. **Acknowledge**. Acknowledge the intention, courage and patience that it takes for each of you to work together in this difficult time.

Take the War Out of Your Words

Most of us have never been taught to use words effectively. Our emotional vocabulary is limited. We have not been shown that words we use can prevent destructive conflict from happening—or pour oil on a fire that is just starting. Learning how to take the war out of your words in communicating about your divorce will not only make your divorce easier but will bring great emotional rewards to you personally.

Author and therapist Sharon Strand Ellison has devoted her life to work in this area. Her book, *Taking the War Out of Our Words*, takes us to the root of our communication problems: defensiveness. She outlines six basic patterns we use: self-betrayal, avoidance, sabotage, vindictiveness, excuses, and blame.[4] She also talks about the costs of defensiveness in our relationships and the problems it creates, as well as how to eliminate your own defensiveness to open up communication. In Ellison's book, she describes three basic misuses in forms of communication:

Questions: Misuses include asking a question to make a statement, to express your own opinion, to entrap someone, to expose

---

[4] I recommend visiting Ellison's website www.PNDC.com to learn more about Powerful Non-Defensive Communication.

someone or to make them feel bad. In clear communication questions are used to obtain information.

Statements: A misuse of statements might be stating a personal *opinion* as a fact, or using a statement to coerce others to agree. In clear communication, statements of fact are stated just as a statement of a fact. In clear communication when you have an opinion, you preface it with "in my opinion" or "this is what I think."

Predictions: It is a misuse of communication to employ predictions as threats, using potential negative consequences to force someone into doing what you want. The gentler, but still inappropriate, version is the coaxing prediction which is, "if you do this for me, you will probably get the result you want." In clear communication you express what it is you want and ask for what it is you need.

Chapter 7

From Conflict to Resolution

The definition of conflict includes wars, differences in philosophy, opposing goals, even internal psychological struggles—and everything in-between! Some of us are brought up to avoid conflict at all costs. Others are taught that you must always come out "on top" in a conflict. But few of us are taught to handle conflict well. Most of us lack effective conflict-resolution skills, so our reactions to conflict can cause even more hurt and anger than the conflict itself.

When the conflict involves people closest to us, our emotions and defensive reactions are intensified. Add to that the stress and heightened emotions of divorce itself, and you have a sure recipe for potential disaster!

Although conflict in divorce can be highly emotional and runs the full gamut from internal struggles to opposing desires or objectives, you *can* learn to handle it well. Even if you have had a lifelong pattern of feeling unsuccessful in dealing with conflict, you can become skilled at conflict resolution by understanding yourself and your spouse, and learning some communication tools. If you take the time to learn to handle conflict well, you ensure not only that the outcomes (decisions and agreements) of the divorce are optimally beneficial but also that the process itself is easier on everyone involved.

Conflict Styles

Individual people handle conflict differently. Your "conflict style" (and that of your spouse) is a reflection of upbringing and intrinsic personality. The first step in becoming effective in conflict is to understand your unique style and that of your spouse. The following are some basic styles:

Avoidant: The "avoidant" tries to avoid directly confronting the issue at hand. When conflict arises, an avoidant may change the subject or procrastinate by putting off a discussion until later. If she can, she might leave the room or hang up the phone when conflict is brewing. If he is unhappy about something or sees a problem on the horizon, he simply will not bring it up. An avoider hopes that, if he ignores it long enough, the problem will just disappear.

The avoider often feels isolated and alone. He cannot see any way that conflicting agendas can be resolved, and often fears being hurt or hurting someone by trying to engage in the conflict. She generally feels hopeless as soon as conflict arises.

A client of mine, Melanie, was a classic avoider. Each time her husband Ed brought up an issue that Melanie was not ready to face, she would excuse herself and go to the restroom. Upon her return she would claim she was not feeling well and could not continue any further that day. At first, I understood. That level of stress definitely affects the body. But when this happened for a third time during our third session, I knew I needed to help Melanie find her way through her avoidance. I talked to her about it and she agreed to try to stay present in our discussions and face what needed to be faced. But after a few unsuccessful attempts, Ed became impatient. They ended up in a more adversarial process with two separate attorneys who could speak for each of them so that Melanie could continue to personally avoid the conflict.

Accommodator: An accommodator places others' desires and others' viewpoints above their own. They will let others prevail, often without discussion, because their main goal is to keep the peace. Accommodators usually think their ideas are not as worthy as others' ideas, so adopt others' positions without even mentioning their own. Accommodators are willing to sacrifice their own interests and let others prevail because they think it is the best way to show support and maintain the relationship.

An accommodator often ends up feeling disappointed and unappreciated. Because their viewpoints are never brought to the table, they often feel that others have taken advantage of them. They may even get to the point where they do not know what they want or what their own opinions are because they have deferred so often to others.

Tim was a situational accommodator, meaning that he was not a classic accommodator in all situations. But in our initial divorce session, he agreed to everything his wife Elizabeth wanted. I finally asked Tim why he was unable to speak up for what he wanted in this divorce. He said it was his fault the marriage was ending and he felt unworthy of asking Elizabeth for anything. He also hoped that if he gave everything to Elizabeth, she would reconcile with him.

Elizabeth plainly stated she was done with the marriage and would not reconcile. But Tim still felt guilt about his behavior during the marriage and was unable to ask for what he was entitled to. I finally asked Tim what he had done that made him feel so guilty. He admitted he had been sexually unfaithful. It had meant nothing to him but he knew it was wrong. Elizabeth felt she deserved to receive *all* the community assets because of Tim's behavior. Tim could not separate what he had done from what he was legally entitled to. I recommended that both Tim and Elizabeth go to different individual counselors to work through the guilt and the anger before proceeding any further with the divorce process.

Adversary: An adversary is competitive and wants to control the conflict so that she ends up "on top." Any hint of conflict brings her hackles up and she is ready to do battle! He may nip conflict in the bud by forcefully insisting that his way is the one and only right way. An adversary can be very rigid. She feels that she *must* win, so she will apply pressure and coercion when necessary.

At the end of the day, an adversary is a tired warrior who feels alone. He feels a constant pressure to be on guard and attack if threatened—whether these threats are real or imagined. The stress of being an adversary can lead to addiction and more serious personal problems.

James was a trial attorney and definitely played the adversary in his divorce. He was not about to agree to anything, no matter how reasonable or fair. When his wife Susan attempted to explain to James how important it was for her to stay in the family residence for the children's sake, he had a counter argument: "The kids don't need the house. They need their mom to get a job." Susan had been a stay-at-home mother for the last seventeen years and her youngest of four children was only three years old. James did not seem to care. He was determined to argue about everything, but Susan remained firm because of her dedication as a mother and determination to do what was best for her children. Finally, after several weeks, James wore himself out. He came up with a compromise that would allow Susan to stay in the house if she took on a part-time job. She agreed, knowing that part-time work would still give her time with the children while preparing her for full-time work later.

Compromiser: A conflict compromiser believes everyone has to give up something. She has to give up something to get what she needs—and so does he. A compromiser wants to reach an easy, fast agreement to avoid the pain. He wants to just split the difference and move on. To compromisers, "meeting half-way" is the only path to resolution. She assumes that both parties must lose something to end the conflict.

A compromiser ends up feeling dissatisfied and discouraged. He thinks that it is only "fair" that both parties lose to resolve the conflict, but still ends up feeling unhappy about the results.

My client Nancy was a compromiser. Initially, she was willing to compromise and give her retirement savings to her husband Bill to buy him out of the family residence. This could have been a great idea, but every time Nancy discussed the details, she complained it was unfair. She would end up with no money to retire with, but what was Bill losing in the deal? She needed to see Bill sacrifice something valuable as well. She could not see that he was forfeiting his interest in the family home. She could only see her own sacrifice of her retirement funds.

Collaborative: A collaborative is a creative problem-solver who sees that two heads are better than one. She believes "fairness" means that both parties speak freely and clearly about their interests and needs. A collaborative will assert his own views, yet will be interested in hearing the other party's views before reaching any conclusions. A collaborative is relatively comfortable in conflict, seeing conflict as a natural and neutral way to process information and differing interests. She welcomes differences as an opportunity to generate more options and solutions. A collaborative wants to search for solutions that will meet all the concerns, interests and needs, ultimately creating a mutually satisfying agreement.

A collaborative recognizes and accepts there will be tension in the conflict and the relationship when parties have contrasting viewpoints. But he trusts that these differences will be worked out much more completely and result in a better solution when both parties have participated.

At the end of the day, a collaborative feels a sense of accomplishment and satisfaction. She feels respected and respectful of her partner. He feels confident that the solutions created in collaboration with the other person will be sustainable and mutually beneficial.

Linda and Tim wrote a vision/mission statement about what they wanted from their collaborative divorce. Their vision statement stated:

We begin this process with the best of intentions for one another. Our lives came together with love, promise and determination but now we have gone on separate paths. We will honor these separate paths for the sake of our children, for ourselves, our families and friends. We acknowledge the significant changes and loss we are experiencing and the impact on each of us and our family and friends.

We appreciate the respect we have for one another and will honor this respect by taking care in our continued interactions in and out of the divorce process. We will work together with dignity and integrity to arrive at a mutually agreeable settlement. We will be impeccable with our word.

We will strive to maintain harmony and share special family moments together.

Tim and Linda read this mission statement to their entire team at the beginning of each of the collaborative divorce meetings. Their collaborative team consisted of Tim and Linda, plus their two divorce coaches (who helped them to create their mission statement), the two collaborative attorneys, and their joint financial specialist. Tim and Linda were impeccable with their word as they each did what was necessary to provide the information needed to move their case forward collaboratively. They have both been a wonderful referral source because they were, and still are, committed to the collaborative process as the only way to obtain a divorce.

Is it obvious which conflict style I prefer? Honestly, I think the collaborative style produces the best results with the least amount of stress. Even if you do not adopt the collaborative style forever, I think you will be well-served to adopt it during the process of your divorce.

However, you need to start where you are and understand your own pattern. In which conflict style did you see yourself? What results has that style produced for you in life so far? How do you feel about yourself and others when you have handled conflict that way?

What about your spouse? What is his or her style? How have your conflict styles played out in your marriage? Do you think you two could deal with conflict differently and produce more positive results?

This book will not teach you how to change others and their conflict style. But change will automatically happen when *you* change. For example, if you choose to be less adversarial, it is likely that your spouse will feel less defensive. If you start expressing opinions and ideas that you have kept hidden, your spouse will probably gain a new understanding of you and your perspective. If you adopt a more collaborative style, your spouse will feel respected and will experience more trust in the negotiation process.

Why Collaborate?

If you are not totally convinced to follow the collaborative route, let me offer a few more thoughts:

Work together because conflict is *much* more expensive. The average divorce in America costs $43,000. This figure does not include couples with high incomes (whose divorces can exceed a million dollars!) or the cost of returning to courts later to modify child-support payments or settle disputes that were not addressed collaboratively in the initial settlement.

Fortunately, you can control the costs by working together. Even though divorce is painful and you may not feel inclined to cooperate, it is usually in your best interests to do so. You will save a lot of money—money you will need and want to start a new life— if you and your spouse can work together.

Determine your priorities and set realistic goals. It is always helpful to begin the divorce process with a realistic end in sight. Before you meet with a mediator or an attorney, take time to list your priorities and goals. In the long run, what is *really* important to you? What things are nice but not necessary? What is the best outcome you can imagine? What is the absolute least you could settle for? Before you begin the process, be clear with yourself about your priorities for yourself and your children. If you are one of the rare divorcing couples who can do this together, great. If not, it is still helpful that you each individually get clear.

Do NOT withhold information from your spouse. To achieve a complete and fair agreement, it is essential that you both fully disclose all of the assets and debts of the marriage, as well as your separate assets and debts. Hiding assets is against the law and will hurt you in the long run. The law considers the marriage relationship to be a fiduciary relationship that carries with it special rules of obligation and trust. The fiduciary duties continue until the divorce is final.

In a famous California Case, a woman named Denise Rossi won $1.3 million in the California State Lottery in 1996. She concealed the winnings from her husband of 25 years and filed for a divorce eleven days after she realized she had won. Two years after the divorce was finalized, her ex-husband discovered she had won the lottery. He took her to court and the judge gave the entire $1.3 million in winnings to the husband, because of Mrs. Rossi's dishonesty and breach of fiduciary duties. Even if you have not won the lottery, concealing assets is not worth the risk.

Conflict can be valuable if it is approached collaboratively. In collaborative conflict resolution, the central goal is to find solutions through *constructive* exchange. The feelings around divorce can make that constructive exchange more challenging. One of the keys to collaboration and constructive exchange is learning to listen.

Mindful Inquiry

The next step in becoming a collaborative is to learn how to use "mindful inquiry" to gather information. Remember that a collaborative resolves conflict through *opening up to information.* And the best way to gather information is to inquire.

Inquiry can be defined as any process that augments knowledge, resolves doubt, or gathers intelligence to solve a problem. All of this is necessary to reach a mutually beneficial divorce-settlement agreement. Inquiry and gathering information is also important to resolve conflict that hampers the settlement process. I have seen many conflicts that existed just because one or both parties lacked information. In these cases, once the inquiry was made and the information obtained, the conflict resolved itself.

Inquiry in general is good and helpful, but I have found that the form of inquiry that leads to the most successful divorce outcomes is *mindful* inquiry. Mindful inquiry is based on the characteristics of mindfulness itself: alert attention without judgment. In mindful inquiry, you gather all the information you need to make decisions during the divorce process, such as: information about what you, your spouse and your children need and want; your current and anticipated financial status; and the options and possibilities for resolving various issues.

The first mindful inquiry practice you will do is to make a written inquiry with yourself. List clearly what you know and what you do not know about your divorce. This may range from financial information to the desires of your children. From there, build a list of mindful inquiry questions to examine for yourself and to bring to your divorce discussions, such as:

- When will you and your spouse move apart?

- How will you share your children's time when you move apart?

- Once separated, what will you do with the family residence?

- How shall you divide the household furniture and property?

- How will you divide your retirement funds?

- What are the tax consequences of various decisions and options?

- How will you divide the debts? The income?

- How much money do each of you need in order to live apart?

The use of mindful inquiry may be helpful in confirming or diminishing any concerns you have. I have also seen conflict resolved when one person took the time to inquire and examine the truth about an assumption they were making.

Interest-Based Divorce Negotiation

Interest-based negotiation has been practiced for years in many settings by various names. I first learned of it as win-win negotiation when I sold real estate. Other terms I have heard used include mutual-gain negotiation, principle-based negotiation, problem-solving negotiation, or best-practice or integrative bargaining.

In the divorce process, professionals have come to prefer the term "interest-based negotiation." By applying the interest-based principles, we strive to understand and determine the interests and possibilities of everyone in the process. No matter what we call it, the intent is to offer parties more flexibility than traditional court-based divorce negotiation. The goal is to avoid locking the two parties into predetermined issues and bargaining positions. Instead, the process begins with understanding the issue and identifying the interests that underlie each side's problems and positions.

When everyone understands the interests and concerns that lead a person to take a position on an issue, they often find that some of those interests are mutual, and that both spouses are trying to achieve the same goal though they are taking different approaches. Clients frequently discover that what at first appear to be competing interests are not really competing at all. Dealing with each other through interest-based negotiation makes it possible to generate and consider options to satisfy particular interests that may never have been considered before.

Principles of Interest-Based Bargaining. Parties who participate in interest-based negotiation realize that the resulting agreements address issues in more depth than those reached using traditional techniques. This is because the process is aimed at satisfying mutual interests by consensus, not just one side's interests at the expense of the other. When spouses deal with each other from this perspective, the results usually go beyond immediate issues to address long-term interests and concerns.

Interest-based bargaining is a process that encourages parties to become joint problem-solvers. It assumes that mutual gain is possible, that solutions which satisfy mutual interests are more durable, and that the parties should help each other achieve a positive result. Interest-based discussions assume that negotiation, like other aspects of the process, can enhance the relationship, and that decisions based on mutual interests reduce or eliminate the need to rely on power plays. Interest-based negotiation is built on several principles for meaningful problem solving:

- Sharing relevant information is critical for effective solutions.

- Focus on issues, not personalities.

- Focus on the present and future, not the past.

- Focus on the interests underlying the issues.

- Focus on mutual interests, and helping to satisfy the other party's interests as well as your own.

When dealing with conflict, it is important to distinguish *interest-based motives* from *position-based motives*. The distinction may seem subtle at first but one (interest-based motives) leads to productive communication and conflict resolution, while the other (position-based motives) leads to resistance, defensiveness and communication breakdown.

An **interest-based motive** is flexible, accommodating and serves the interest at hand. The delivery of an interest-based motive is often open, friendly, compassionate and concerning. A **position-based motive** is rigid, sometimes vengeful and often self-serving. The delivery of a position-based motive is often bitter, angry and offensive to others. To help you get the distinction, here are several examples:

#1: Maria usually drives her son, Joe, an hour to his father's house every other Saturday morning. If her motivation is **interest-based**, Maria might ask Joe's father, Jose, to change the scheduled drop-off for this Saturday morning because it will be Joe's first chance to play in his team's soccer match. This request is about the interests of their child. But if Maria is **position-based** and focused on the "unfairness" of making the one-hour drive, she would tell Jose that if he wants to see his son this weekend he will have to come pick him up and that because he has a soccer game Saturday morning it will have to be after the game.

#2: In the process of dividing their assets, Don and Patty have to figure out how to handle Don's retirement fund. Coming from a **position-based** stance, Don might say, "It's my retirement. I earned it and I should keep it." But if he came from an **interest-based** place, he might say something like, "How can I keep my retirement and give you something of equal value?"

#3: Anna and Paul have a beautiful home in a great neighborhood that they shared for 15 years. From a **position-based** motive, Anna might say, "I can't even imagine where else I would live so I'm keeping the house." But if she switches to being **interest-based**, she might say, "I'd like to explore the financial possibility of keeping the house and what we can do to make that happen."

#4: Ken and Julia married at an early age and are in their mid-thirties. Ken had been very successful in his career while Julia stayed at home with their young children. If Ken is **position-based** when the subject of spousal support comes up, he might insist, "I don't want to pay you support forever." But if he remains **interest-based**, he might ask, "How can I help you to become financially independent so my support obligation can end sooner?"

Can you see the difference? Most importantly, can you see how the discussions that are **interest-based** would end up being much more productive? When dealing with conflict, ask yourself why this particular issue is important to you before you communicate. What is your motivation? Is it interest-based? Position-based? If it is a combination of the two, can you focus on the motivation that is interest-based and put the position-based portion to the side?

Decision-making Tools

Negotiations are really a string of decisions, aren't they? Some decisions will be yours alone: "How will I deal with my share of the assets?" "What do I need to do to begin this new chapter of my life?" "What kind of parent will I be under this new arrangement?" Other decisions will be joint decisions: "Where will the children be for holidays?" "What assets will we sell?" "How will we communicate going forward?"

Listening and speaking mindfully and from interest-based motivation will assist greatly with all of these decisions. Here are some additional guidelines that will support you in having positive, productive decision-making conversations. It is helpful if both parties follow these guidelines, but if your spouse is resistant, you will still benefit from following them yourself. During decision-making discussions:

- Make sure you understand the *real* issues from both your point of view and theirs;

- Treat disagreement as acceptable and simply part of the process;

- Invite and encourage the other person to present ideas and possible solutions;

- Seriously and sincerely consider the other person's ideas and suggestions;

- Discuss more than just one side of the idea or issue;

- Talk through the advantages, disadvantages, and consequences of each idea with the other person;

- Clarify areas of agreement as well as disagreement;

- Work toward shared decision-making, without either of you acting as the final decider;

- Remind yourself and the other person that you each have a right to think about the issue for a while and decide at a later time;

- Remind yourself and the other person that decisions can be renegotiated at another time if they do not work out as intended;

- Practice decision-making at times when making the decision is not critical.

I cannot think of a better way to close this chapter than by sharing a little wisdom from Don Miguel Ruiz, author of *The Four Agreements*. The four agreements apply to all of life but can be particularly helpful during the challenging process of divorce. These agreements, like most effective life tools, are simple but not always easy. I invite you to incorporate them into the way you approach your divorce.

Agreement #1: Be impeccable with your word. This agreement asks us to be impeccable on many levels. First, is to be impeccable with ourselves, to honor our own truth and who we are. In the midst of making decisions and coming to agreements during your divorce, it is important to keep checking in with yourself: Is this really in alignment with who I am and what I want for my family? Can I make this commitment and stay in integrity?

Next, is to be impeccable in our words and deeds with others. To do what we say we will do and to tell the truth no matter how difficult. In this challenging time, it is especially important that you are trustworthy in your actions and honest in your communications.

Agreement #2: Don't take things personally. What others say and do is a reflection of who *they* are, not who *you* are. You did not *cause* others to do or say anything. You are only responsible for your own words and actions, not anyone else's.

If your spouse says something demeaning or refuses to compromise, remind yourself that it is not about *you*, but a symptom of his or her own fears. If your children become angry and upset, remind yourself that it is not about *you*, but the stress they feel about change and the unknown.

Agreement #3: Don't make assumptions. This agreement encourages us to look beyond what we think we know. To remember that others do not necessarily think the way we do, or value the things we value. To be aware that we do not know why others do the things they do, and that past actions do not necessarily predict future actions.

During your divorce process, be particularly aware of assumptions you make about your spouse. Have the courage to ask questions. Remain curious. As Will Rogers said, "It isn't what we know that gives us trouble. It's what we know that ain't so."

Agreement #4: Always do your best. The decisions you make and agreements you create during your divorce will impact you and your family for many years to come. Give this process your best effort! That means doing your best to release negative emotions so you can think clearly and act appropriately. It means doing your best to listen fully and communicate honestly. It means doing your best to take care of yourself and respect your spouse throughout the process.

Understand that on some days your best will be better than other days—and that is okay. Just do your best to get back on track in whatever way you need.

Chapter 8

Co-Parenting

Your divorce separates you from your spouse in most ways, but if you have children, you are still bound together as parents. Parenting, and especially co-parenting, is a daunting task. It is so important that I wrote an entire book on the subject, *Collaborative Co-parenting*, and developed an online course to assist divorcing parents. I cannot cover all I wrote in just one chapter, but I would like to share some of the points I think are most important for you to consider.

From Marriage Partners to Parenting Partners

Some people find that co-parenting is easy while others struggle to even remain civil with their former spouse. Fortunately, we have many more role models today showing us that parents who were once married *can* get along after divorce. Whether easy or difficult, it is still a transition and a change in your relationship dynamics. Your relationship is transitioning from married, intimate partners to "parenting partners."

Making this change from marriage partners to parenting partners requires focusing on the present and letting go of the past.

As we have discussed throughout this book, you need to start by letting go of blame, regrets, and resentments and resist the urge to fall back into old patterns of arguing or trying to hurt each other. Regrets and anger about the past interfere with your ability to parent positively in the present. A successful parent partnership requires cooperation. Your goal is to support your children's lives, to keep your focus on *them* rather than on your own crises or conflicts you may still have with your ex.

This perspective can make all the difference. A client of mine told her estranged husband that she wanted to get along better because they were going to "be parenting partners forever." Her statement switched on a light in his head, and he instantly became much more cooperative. What these co-parents came to understand was absolutely right: you and your co-parent are going to be parents together for the rest of your lives.

What is a parenting partnership? It is a business-like relationship between two parents who are able to conduct themselves professionally, collaboratively and creatively for the sake of their children. A healthy parenting partnership puts your children's best interests first. This is the foundation for your children to be nourished and supported by *both* parents. You can start by both of you agreeing to form a partnership to *work together* to provide for the emotional and physical needs of your children.

Forming a Successful Parenting Partnership

Once two parents have agreed to form a partnership, it helps to have some guidelines to work within, just as you would with any partnership. You can start with a mission statement, a written statement that captures what your parent partnership is about and why it is important. Your mission statement can keep you both focused on the purpose of your partnership and what is genuinely important to you—the wellbeing of your children. For example, your co-parenting mission statement might be as simple as: *The purpose of our partnership is to ensure the physical and emotional wellbeing of our children to the best of our ability. We will work together in any way necessary to make sure they feel safe, supported and nurtured.*[5]

To help your new co-parenting relationship succeed, it is also helpful to have some basic agreed-upon guidelines in place in advance. You will find that setting these guidelines up *before* sticky situations arise is easier than trying to resolve conflict without any guidelines in place. You probably know your co-parent's hot buttons and he or she knows yours. Try to agree on some guidelines in advance that address these specific problem areas. For example, if your ex is obsessively early and you are always running behind, set a guideline about calling each other when you are going to be more than 15 minutes late.

Here are some other examples of guidelines you might use, but I encourage you to create a personalized list:

- We will not argue in front of our children.

- Children will not be used to transmit messages or money.

- We will not say degrading things about the other parent to our children or in front of our children.

- We will ask our families and friends to avoid saying degrading things about either parent to our children.

- We will limit our children's contact with "toxic" friends or relatives who are not willing to be supportive or who criticize either parent in front of our children.

- If a parent picking up or dropping off a child is going to be more than 15 minutes late, he or she will call to notify the other parent.

- We will both try to accommodate schedule changes needed by the other parent as much as is reasonably possible.

- We will accommodate our children's activities whenever possible so they do not have to change their lives because of divorce.

---

[5] For more information and details about how to write a mission statement, see Chapter 2 of my book *Collaborative Co-parenting*.

- We will work together to create guidelines for raising our child.

- All items taken from one parent's home to the other's household will travel back and forth with the child, especially important items such as sports uniforms, eye glasses, favorite blankets, coats, school books, musical instruments and favorite toys.

- We will check with each other when our child expresses a complaint about one of us in order to hear the adult version.

- We will respect each other's privacy and not use our children as informers or spies.

- We will divide ongoing responsibilities. For example, maybe Dad takes the children for all their haircuts and back-to-school shopping while Mom takes the children to all routine medical and dental checkups.

- We will not discuss emotional issues regarding the breakup or anger at each other with the children.

You might start by each of you drafting a mission statement and list of operating guidelines. Compare your lists and talk them through. To avoid problems in the future, get as specific as you can with one another about your co-parenting expectations.

Talking to Children about Divorce

Talking to your children *together* about the divorce can help establish a positive co-parenting relationship. By doing it this way, you present a united front that says, "We won't be married but we'll always be your parents." Both of you can answer your children's questions and address their concerns. It also helps you both avoid the temptation to place blame for the divorce. Children's reactions are closely tied to how and what parents communicate about the divorce. I urge you to think carefully about the words you use.

The following tips can help you handle not only the first discussion with your children about the breakup, but in later talks as well:

- Talking to your children about the divorce together will give them the reassurance that they are not going to lose one of their parents.

- Do not keep the divorce a secret or wait until the last minute. You do not want your children to find out about the divorce or other significant changes to their lives from some other source.

- Keep things simple and straightforward. Even if they could understand it, children do not have to be burdened with the details of the divorce process.

- Although divorce is a difficult time, it is important for you to be calm and reassuring when discussing the divorce with your children.

- Children often feel they are the cause of the divorce. Let them know the divorce is not their fault. This is a message they will need to hear repeatedly from you.

- Tell your children that you both love them and the divorce will not change your love for them.

- Acknowledge that divorce is sad and upsetting for everyone. It is okay to allow time for the sadness, loss, even anger about the changes taking place.

- Validate their feelings without trying to fix them or trying to talk your children out of what they feel.

- When talking about the divorce, do not discuss the other parent's faults or problems with your children.

- Avoid arguing or discussing financial issues in front of your children.

- Give children opportunities to have a loving, satisfying relationship with both of you.

Children Need Trust

When children know they can count on and trust the people in their lives, they feel secure and self-confident. Parents earn the trust of their children when their words match their actions. If you make a promise, do all you can to follow through on keeping that promise.

Often the changes children witness during divorce are unsettling. They see new emotions and behaviors from their parents, some of which are not pretty. Children who cannot trust their parents to behave calmly and responsibly will have trouble trusting that everything after the divorce will eventually be okay. Your charged emotional state or negative behaviors will be confusing and upsetting to children. To minimize their upset, practice solid co-parenting skills that shield children from the more negative aspects of divorce. Stay constant in following the mission statement you wrote and adhering to the guidelines you created.

Building Trust as Co-Parents

Trust is important in any relationship, so it makes sense that you and your co-parent must find a way to rebuild trust in this new partnership. If one parent feels that the other is withholding or distorting information, trust in the co-parenting relationship will break down. One way to build trust is to keep the agreements and promises you make to one another.

Imagine business partners failing to share important information about the ups and downs of their business or failing to do what they committed to do in the company. This would be devastating to the company's success. That kind of behavior will damage your parenting partnership just as much. Trust is key to building a successful partnership.

"But what about my co-parent and all the things he or she has done in the past?" You can never control how another person behaves, but you can control your own behavior. Just one person can provide the foundation for a business-like relationship. Your trustworthiness and sincere cooperation can make all the difference in building a positive co-parent partnership. It may take time to rebuild trust so you can be good partners for your children. Be patient.

Focus on the big picture, not minor disagreements or inconveniences. Just remember, although disagreements occur in every partnership, how you handle these differences is what determines success. Many of my clients are visibly relieved when I advise them to view the relationship with their co-parent as a business relationship instead of a friendship. A business relationship is the ideal model for working together to make choices in the best interests of your children after a divorce or breakup. You would not let minor differences or irritations with a business partner keep you from achieving a shared goal. When it comes to your family, keep your children and their needs as your focus. Following through on your partnering commitments *despite* your disagreements will help you as much as it benefits your children.

Business partnerships are often built by bringing different talents together. Differences have value. Great ideas and innovation in business are usually developed by the creative contributions of a diverse group of people with unique personality types and skill sets. You and your co-parenting partner also bring different assets to the table. Learn to value one another's differences. These differences may have driven you apart as a married couple, but now they can be useful in your parenting partnership.

Good business partners also learn to accept conflict, differing opinions, and contrary perspectives. If they are smart, they work through conflict with the understanding that there is always more than one way to do things.

Honoring Differences

There was a time when children who were born left-handed were encouraged to use their right hands instead because it was believed to be the "correct" choice. As you can imagine, these now-corrected children ended up struggling to function, write and do basic day-to-day activities because they were going against their natural left-handedness. Just as being left-handed is natural for some and *not* inferior to being right-handed, one parenting style is not better than another style. They are simply different.

Because no two people are alike, it stands to reason that no two parents are exactly alike either. Each of us has a unique personality that makes our parenting style different from other people's styles. Not realizing this leads many parents into conflict because they tend to expect the other parent to parent the same way they do. However, there are numerous, equally valuable ways to parent children. Acknowledging this will make your co-parenting partnership much smoother.

Children need both their parents' gifts. One parenting style is not more important than the other. Recognizing the differences in your personalities and parenting styles is the first step. The second step—which is a big one—is to honor the best of each style and acknowledge each as beneficial to your children's wellbeing and growth.

Valuing differences will also help you become more flexible. Notice if you find yourself being too picky, critical, or demanding. The real issue might simply be that your co-parent's style is different from your own. Ask yourself, "Is this difference really harmful to our children, or is it just not how I prefer to do things?" Pressuring your co-parent to adapt to your own style because you simply prefer it can be invasive and lead to unnecessary conflict and resentment. In addition, it sends a confusing message to your children, making them doubt themselves or you as their parents.

Pick your battles and let small concerns or irritations pass. Instead, focus on major issues that concern your children's health, safety, education and welfare. Letting go of the frustration of minor differences can be freeing. Finding the place where these differences can be complementary, rather than conflicting, is the goal of collaborative co-parenting.[6]

Do This for Your Children

When getting along seems difficult, keep in mind that you are doing all of this for your children. All children deserve to feel secure. All children deserve to feel loved. Making your co-parenting partnership work well helps children see that they still have two parents and a real family.

---

[6] I have dedicated an entire chapter to understanding differences in my book, *Collaborative Co-parenting*. I recommend you take a look at this to more deeply understand the value of differences.

Chapter 9

Divorce Process Options

Once you have decided to divorce, the option you select regarding how you will get your divorce is probably the single most significant choice you will make.

In a traditional divorce, each party retains an attorney and the attorneys negotiate the divorce, either privately or, if necessary, in front of a judge. This process is generally the most expensive, time-consuming and emotionally draining option. But you have other options you can consider: mediation, collaborative divorce, settlement-oriented divorce, or self-representation. These different alternative dispute resolution (ADR) or consensual dispute resolution (CDR) options give you more control over the decisions you make and how you make them. They can also save you time, money and stress.

Choosing the best option for your divorce depends on a number of factors, such as motivation to come to mutually beneficial solutions (or not), the level of contentiousness of the divorce, the ability to disagree constructively, each party's ability to speak up for themselves, the level of trust or mistrust between the parties, and how realistic each party's expectations are.

The other question to consider is whether you and your spouse can agree on the appropriate divorce option. If you do not agree initially, some attorneys would tell you that litigation is your only option. But I disagree. In my experience, if one of you thoroughly researches the options and shares that information with the other, you can often find that the other party is willing to explore the options with you. For example, hundreds of couples have come to me after reviewing the information and insight I offer on my web-site (www.FamilyLawCenter.US). You can also interview attorneys and mediators before making a decision to get clearer about your options—and consultation rates with these professionals are often lower than their regular hourly rate.

Mediation

Mediation is a process in which a qualified mediator acts as a neutral third party to help you reach a settlement in your legal issues. The role of the mediator is to guide your discussion, explore settlement alternatives and resolve difficult conflicts. I have been providing divorce mediation services for over twenty years, and my clients have found it to be very beneficial and rewarding.[7]

The mediation I am describing here is private, all-inclusive mediation. There is also a type of "mediation" that is performed by "court mediators." Court mediators handle custody issues only and are not typically confidential.

In the mediation process, you and your spouse meet togeth-er with your chosen mediator in private mediation sessions (the number of sessions depends on the complexity of issues and your readiness to resolve them). The two of you exchange necessary in-formation and discuss ideas about how to settle your differences. Your mediator will explain the law as it pertains to your situation, including property division and the calculation of child and spousal support. In this process, you and your spouse make the decisions

---

[7] For more information on Divorce Mediation, I highly recommend obtaining Gary Friedman's book *Divorce Mediation* or visit his website www.UnderstandingInConflict. org The Center for Understanding in Conflict.

together. Although your mediator may provide guidance, a mediator's main function is to facilitate your decision-making process.

Advantages of Mediation

- Mediation allows the parties to obtain legal information from a *neutral,* non-adversarial independent attorney.

- Mediation is typically less expensive than other options, making it economically feasible for most couples.

- Mediation reduces the fears associated with divorce or legal separation.

- Mediation does not require any court appearances and therefore keeps financial matters private.

- Mediation avoids the polarization and hostility that often result from court proceedings.

- Mediation allows the parties direct involvement in the decision-making process.

- Mediation allows the parties to move at a mutually agreeable pace, usually taking a fraction of the time compared to court proceedings.

- Mediation establishes a level of communication and cooperation between the parties that is mutually beneficial in the future.

- Mediation assists divorcing parents to transition from marital partners to parenting partners.

- Mediation incorporates a parenting plan that accommodates everyone's best interest, especially the children.

A mediator is typically an attorney, however in the role of mediator he/she is not acting as an attorney for either party, nor is he/she acting as an attorney for both parties. Instead, your mediator's role is to provide each party, in the presence of the other, with the information necessary to allow them to make informed decisions regarding legal issues.

Not everyone can mediate. There are cases that cannot and do not belong in mediation. A good mediator can help you determine if you and your spouse are able to mediate. In cases of severe domestic violence and or severe emotional abuse, the psychological dysfunction and inequality are so great that even a good mediator cannot balance the power between the spouses. If there is not severe physical or emotional abuse in your relationship, I recommend you take the time to find a qualified mediator and go for at least one session to help determine if you and your spouse are candidates for mediation.

Even if there has not been severe physical or emotional abuse, divorce mediation is not right for everyone. If one or both parties lack the motivation to mediate, or if you are not able to speak up for yourselves, or if your mistrust level of one another is high, other options may be preferable.

When you and your spouse are motivated to work together in the mediation process and produce results that are *mutually* beneficial, the process can be highly successful. Without that motivation, it can be difficult, if not impossible, to mediate. Both of you must also be willing to speak up for yourselves and to assert your concerns and desires; mediation is *not* about capitulating to each other. You may not be skilled at speaking up for yourselves initially. But if you are willing to get better at it, a good mediator will be instrumental in helping both of you speak up and listen to one another when challenges or conflicts arise.

The greater the level of trust there is between you and your spouse, the greater likelihood that the mediation will be successful. If the trust between the two of you has been shattered—or was never present in the first place—it is very difficult to have productive discussions about the issues you will need to resolve. A skilled mediator can help you process issues of trust and help you see how or if they are directly related to the decisions that need to be made. But again, both parties must at least be *willing* to trust one another to the level necessary to negotiate constructively.

Willingness to let go of the past and be in the present is critical to a successful mediation. It is natural to feel pain or anger about the breakup and what may have led to it. However, a successful mediation requires you both to work through those emotions or at least put them to the side as you work through the issues at hand. Your decisions and agreements need to be based on the *present as well as future needs*, not muddied with compromises based on guilt or uncompromising positions based on the desire for revenge.

To be successful in mediation, you both must be realistic about what you want and expect from each other in the settlement agreement and in the mediation process. Mediation is not a process that encourages taking advantage of your spouse. A skilled mediator will guide a fair and balanced exchange so that both of you have realistic expectations and reach an equitable settlement.

Collaborative Divorce

Collaborative practice is a new way to resolve conflicts in a respectful and mutually agreed-upon process. The clients do not sign a settlement agreement until each of them is comfortable with it. All information is voluntarily shared as soon as possible. Everyone agrees to operate with good faith efforts to explore options central to the divorce process.

In a collaborative process, each spouse has his/her own family law attorney. Everyone—including the attorneys—commit to resolving differences in a manner acceptable to both parties in a comfortable environment, without the threat of resorting to the court system or litigation. When issues about children are part of the process, the children's needs are placed first. Clients are active members of a collaborative working team of professionals who provide information and help clients explore a variety of solutions. Each member of the team brings a unique expertise to the process. Interdisciplinary teams enhance the likelihood of achieving the best results for you and your family.

The collaborative process provides a family with more resources, information and support than any of the other options. Although the cost may be more than mediation, it is often much less expensive than an adversarial process that ends up in court. If this option is financially feasible for you, the many benefits of this process greatly outweigh its costs.

In a collaborative process, spouses and their attorneys meet for informal discussions and conferences to settle the issues. A collaborative process strives to maximize settlement options for the benefit of both parties and children, and minimize or eliminate negative economic, social and emotional impacts that occur in litigation.

Advantages of Collaborative Process

- Open and honest exchange of information – In a collaborative process, *all* of the participants agree to an open, honest exchange of accurate information and any necessary documentation. This process reduces cost, expands exploration of creative solutions and creates a collaborative working environment.

- Custody – In a collaborative process, spouses agree to protect their children and not involve them in disputes. They agree to speak respectfully *to* each other and *about* each other in the presence of their children. Spouses negotiate and agree upon parenting decisions, rather than looking to the court to make these decisions. They use a child specialist to help determine what is in the children's best interests.

- Divorce and Communication Coach – Typically, each party has a divorce communication coach to help manage emotions and articulate or reframe their desired needs and wishes.

- Joint experts – In a collaborative process, spouses jointly choose and employ any accountant, appraiser, or other consultant whose services may be required, instead of each separately hiring his or her own adversarial expert. The parties use a joint neutral financial specialist who gathers and organizes the financial information. This not only reduces the costs but keeps the parties from hiring specialists with competing interests.

- Negotiations – In a collaborative process, each spouse acknowledges the other's legitimate needs. They work together creatively for mutual benefit, rather than seeking individual advantages.

- Attorney's role – In collaborative practice, attorneys are committed to the cooperative resolution of all issues. A collaborative practice attorney will withdraw from participation if his or her client abandons the collaborative process or refuses to follow collaborative guidelines.

How the Collaborative Team Works

A typical collaborative team consists of the two parties, two collaborative attorneys, a divorce communication coach for each party and a joint neutral financial specialist. The team works together to establish emotional support for both parties, provide legal information, settlement guidance, and assist the parties to create a mutually beneficial agreement, without having to go to court. The professionals making up the Collaborative team agree to disqualify themselves from any possible future litigation to avoid any potential conflicts of interest. While the team concept may seem to be expensive, in actuality, the team is more efficient and often reduces normal legal fees associated with a litigated divorce.

Collaborative practice is on the cutting edge of improving the process for obtaining a divorce. In 1998, I joined seventeen other attorneys to form a collaborative practice group known as

Sacramento Collaborative Practice Group (SCPG). We now have over 110 members including mental-health professionals and financial specialists as well as legal experts. We are part of the Collaborative Practice California (CPCal) and the International Academy of Collaborative Professionals (IACP).[8] I recommend that you refer to the IACP website (www.CollaborativePractice.com) to find a qualified collaborative team in your area. Also, take a look at www.DivorceOption.com for interesting articles and information about the Collaborative Process.

Settlement-Oriented Representation

Settlement-oriented legal representation is for divorcing spouses who want to work with separate attorneys dedicated solely to advocacy from each client's point of view, yet who still pursue settlement through consensual negotiation.

Family law issues can be complex and emotionally charged. When the trust is not present but you desire to work together in a respectful manner, the settlement-oriented style divorce is certainly better than an adversarial divorce. A settlement-oriented divorce includes settlement negotiations outside of court as well as formal orders in court. In a settlement-oriented representation, you never give up your right to go to court with your chosen attorney.

Ted and Jacqueline had been married for 18 years. Ted was a struggling new attorney when he met Jacqueline who was in her second year of college as a design major. When Jacqueline became pregnant she gladly dropped out of school to obtain her Mrs. Degree rather than a degree in design. At first Ted was concerned about Jacqueline not finishing school, but it didn't take long before he was grateful to have Jacqueline maintain the home front and take care of what turned into three children while he pursued his career. Ted became a sharp business attorney as well as a successful entrepreneur. He formed a partnership with a business

---

[8] You will find much information on the groups' websites; SCPG www.divorceoption.com; CPCal www.CPCal.com; IACP www.CollaborativePractice.com

associate to build a software company. Ted brought the legal skills and his partner brought the technical skills. The company took off almost immediately to become a multimillion dollar firm overnight. It all seemed too good to be true when Jacqueline found out that Ted had been unfaithful with a mutual friend. It was a devastating blow to Jacqueline—not only did she feel betrayed by Ted but also felt betrayed by her friend.

Jacqueline called another friend Pam who had gone through a difficult divorce just a couple of years earlier and had interviewed many attorneys around town. Pam told Jacqueline she needed to hire Attorney Steve, as he was the best, a Certified Family Law Specialist and fellow of the American Academy of Matrimonial Lawyers. Pam told Jacqueline, "Steve will take care of you—it will be expensive, but worth it." Within a week Jacqueline hired Attorney Steve and paid him a retainer of $20,000.

Ted was surprised when Jacqueline told him she was filing for a divorce. He regretted what had happened, still loved Jacqueline and did not want the marriage to end. He pleaded with her to go to counseling but instead found himself staring at divorce papers sent to him with a cordial letter from Attorney Steve. It was hard for Ted to determine what to do or how to fight back because what he really wanted was his family. Being an attorney, Ted decided to call Attorney Steve to determine if he was going to be reasonable or not. The conversation went well, but Attorney Steve recommended that Ted obtain his own attorney. One of Ted's attorney friends who was familiar with Attorney Steve recommended he choose an attorney from the Association of Certified Family Law Specialists. He told Ted that his case was likely to be complicated due to the business interests and high assets and it would best be handled by attorneys who have the experience to manage this kind of case and are equally experienced. Ted interviewed a few of the best family law attorneys and decided on Attorney Mary. She was professional, bright, and well-credentialed. Mary had previous experience dealing with Attorney Steve and felt confident she could manage any conflicts that may arise.

Attorney Mary and Attorney Steve were able to reach settlement agreements on many issues and to informally exchange information and work together professionally with only a few court appearances. The big challenge the two attorneys had was that they did not see eye-to-eye on the value of Ted's business interest in the software company and the amount of compensation he was receiving for support purposes. The attorneys had each hired a different forensic accountant and the two professionals did not agree. This created conflict that was difficult to resolve without a third party opinion.

This was a classic case where the settlement-oriented representation was probably the best option. It provided Jacqueline with what she needed in that she had lost trust in Ted and was not in a frame of mind to believe much he had to say. She had no experience in the business world and felt a total sense of unequal bargaining power. Being represented by Attorney Steve, she was confident that she was going to receive what she was entitled to.

The case went on for two-and-a-half years. Just before the scheduled trial date, Attorney Steve and Attorney Mary reached a full settlement in a professional and respectful manner. Jacqueline and Ted were both relieved and able to move on with their lives.

Adversarial Divorce

Sometimes adversarial divorce is necessary. In an adversarial divorce your attorney will represent only *you* and he or she will aggressively litigate on your behalf.

When the breakup of a marriage is traumatic due to domestic or emotional abuse, it is often necessary to become more aggressive to get a settlement that protects your interests. In the adversarial process, a judge makes all or almost all of the decisions because the parties are unable to reach agreements. This process requires more formal discovery such as depositions, interrogatories (a formal form of asking questions) as well as court appearances. In an adversarial divorce, the attorneys do most of the communicating. An adversarial attorney will usually recommend that their client have minimal or no contact with the other party except what is necessary to implement the child-custody court orders.

Many divorces begin from adversarial positions to obtain the initial temporary court orders. Once the initial trauma of the marriage breakup has settled down, the situation often becomes less adversarial. At that point, parties may be able to complete the divorce in a cooperative manner.

James and Mary came to me for mediation after their first court appearance where they had two separate attorneys and had obtained support and custody court orders. The fear Mary had about how she would support herself had somewhat dissipated now she had a support order. For James, his fear around having time with their children had dissipated because the custody court order gave him a regular parent schedule. The two of them were now glad to move forward with a neutral mediator to settle the property division. The mediated property settlement saved them time, money and additional emotional conflict and trauma. It also allowed them to get back on a cooperative working manner which helped them establish a more collaborative co-parenting partnership.

Self-Representation

Though this is technically an option, I never recommend it. First of all, you are rarely in an emotional state of mind to handle all of the issues involved in divorce. The courts have made the divorce process complex and I have seen too many cases of self-representation that later required some type of correction—or even mistakes which cannot later be corrected. If you do want to be self-represented, please use the services of attorneys who offer limited-scope services to give you guidance and their legal expertise advice in the complexities of the Family Court systems.

Divorce Options Workshop

Collaborative Practice California (CPCal) offers a Divorce Options Workshop that I highly recommend. After attending the Divorce Options Workshops, participants have commented that they feel empowered to make a more informed decision regarding their divorce process choice. Divorce Options Workshops, started by the Sacramento Collaborative Practice Group, are now held throughout California (www.CPCal/DivorceOptions.com) and are being expanded nationwide.

Choosing the Right Professional Team

The right team can make all the difference in how smoothly your divorce process goes and what results you achieve through it. This is a time when you need competent support, professionals you can trust to know what they are doing. Your legal professionals are important but often you need to start with the support of mental-health professionals to assist you and your children cope with the trauma of the breakup of your marriage.

Many of my clients are referred to me by mental-health professionals. When this is the case, often the couple has had time to grieve the loss of the marriage through counseling and both spouses are more ready to proceed with their divorce. Couples who spend time working through emotional issues in counseling often have the easiest and least expensive divorces. Divorce can be extremely painful, especially when the divorce was not a mutual decision. Counseling can help you and your spouse heal old wounds, and prepare for what lies ahead. Doing so will help reduce much of the angst in dealing with the divorce and help you make decisions about family and financial issues.

Finding the Right Mental-Health Professional

Finding the right professional for you or a loved one can be a critical ingredient in the process of dealing with life's challenges.

Referrals from a family law attorney, a friend or a family member are a good starting place.

Therapists: There are many different styles of therapists from cognitive behaviorists to psychoanalysts. Finding the right fit may require a little research. You can ask for preliminary interviews with a few mental-health professionals to get a better understanding of who they are and what each provides. Ask them about their training, their specialties, and how long they have been practicing. You can also go on the website of the state in which they are licensed to see if there have been any past complaints.

Divorce/Communication Coaches: A coach is a licensed mental-health professional who does not act as a therapist but has been specially trained to work with you during divorce as your communication coach. A divorce/communication coach is part of the overall professional team and understands the dynamics of your divorce case. The coach is someone you can talk to about emotions that are coming up and how to manage these emotions and triggers. Coaches can help you speak up for yourself by helping you frame a way to express your desires or to address issues of concern.

Child specialists: Child specialists help children express their feelings and reactions to the divorce and family issues. Child specialists then use this information to help parents better understand their children and meet their needs.

Finding the Right Legal Representation

Of course, the legal representation you choose depends on the process you have chosen. Though technically all qualified Family Law attorneys can represent you in any of the processes, from mediation or collaborative divorce to litigation, the truth is that attorneys specialize and have specific talents, experience and preferences that make them more suitable for certain processes than others.

As you interview prospective attorneys, ask them about their training, experience, and attitudes about divorce. Describe your circumstances and listen to their suggestions about how you should proceed. Trust your instincts: Does this person reflect the approach you would like to take? Do they listen well? Do you feel comfortable communicating with them?

When choosing a Divorce or Family Law attorney, level of experience is vital to most people. I believe that attribute is developed over time. Learning the ropes, knowing local court procedures, and familiarity with other counsel and judges can make a significant difference in representing you in your divorce. It is also important that your attorney has a well-trained professional staff since a busy family law attorney will often be at court.

As in finding other professionals, the best way to find a good family law attorney is through referrals. Ask friends and family who have used family law attorneys and who are satisfied with the results achieved. Or ask a mental-health professional to recommend a family law attorney. Most states have family law attorneys who have taken a second bar exam and received a credential as a Certified Family Law Specialist. Check the listings in your state. Review the State Bar website to be sure the attorney has had no complaints or is under any restrictions. Check to see if the attorney is listed with the Better Business Bureau. Interview several attorneys and ask them what they think about some of their colleagues. Look for a family law attorney on the IACP website, (www. CollaborativePractice.com). These attorneys are all well-trained not only in collaborative law but also in substantive family law and many of them still appear in court in traditional divorce cases.

Mediators: Divorce mediation has evolved significantly since I began over twenty years ago and has become a much more familiar option for divorce. A well-qualified and skilled mediator can help you determine if you are ready or right for mediation.

I recommend you use an attorney who has *significant* experience as a mediator. To find a well-qualified attorney/mediator, ask for a referral from your friends or professional colleagues, or from mental-health professionals, accountants and lawyers who practice in other areas. Ask prospective candidates how long they have been mediating and how much of their practice is dedicated to mediation. (Some attorneys claim to be mediators but only actually mediate one or two cases a year.) Ask if they have any other credentials such as training in mental health, taxes, or other specialties that could be helpful.

Collaborative Attorney: Collaborative practice is a relatively new way to resolve conflicts in divorce, so your contacts may not be able to refer you to one. Collaborative attorneys work only as settlement specialists, and disputing parties will need to hire other lawyers if any of the parties want to litigate. A good resource for finding an attorney who specializes in collaborative practice is the International Academy of Collaborative Professionals (IACP) which has a list of well-trained collaborative attorneys on their websites, (www.CollaborativePractice.com) and (www.CPCal.com).

Keeping Legal Costs Down

As I mentioned previously, trying to handle your divorce entirely by yourself without a legal professional is *not* the best way to keep costs down! The do-it-yourselfer does not typically have expertise or experience to handle the complex settlement issues of divorce in a way that best serves all parties. That said, the more you do yourself, the less you will have to pay an attorney to do.

Prior to your first consultation, ask what information you should bring to help the attorney understand your situation. Some attorneys provide a written list of documents clients need to bring, such as recent pay stubs, income-tax returns, copies of deeds, and Kelly Blue Book estimates on vehicles. Most attorneys charge by the hour, so the better prepared you are, the more affordable your meeting will be. If you happen to have an existing case with the court, bring copies of any documents that have been filed. If you have misplaced these documents, you can go to the court to obtain a copy from your file. Providing this information at your consultation will go a long way toward an effective and efficient consultation.

It is also a good idea to write down your questions and concerns in advance. This way you can cover everything you need to talk about without having to schedule numerous meetings or repeatedly call back with questions.

After your initial consultation, you will need to create an inventory of your property and debts. This does not mean listing every teaspoon, but it does mean listing all large assets and placing an overall value on your assets. Provide paperwork for property that you will be listing, such as statements for investment accounts and current figures for credit-card balances.

Don't pay lawyers to divide your pots and pans! If attorneys have to help you work out who will get the furniture and the wedding china, they may end up charging more than the cost of replacing everything. Here are some ideas on how to divide your personal property:

- **Meet Halfway Method:** Divide financial assets (bank accounts, stocks and bonds, and so on) equally between each party.

- **Balanced Method:** One party takes an entire lot of furniture while the other party takes the car.

- **Easy-as-Pie Method:** One party prepares two lists that divide the assets equally and then the other party gets to choose which list he or she wants. It is important to try to keep sets together (furniture, tables and chairs, bedroom sets, et cetera). This approach can be very helpful for short-term marriages where wedding gifts need to be divided.

- **Divide-and-Conquer Method:** One party places a monetary value on each community item and the other chooses which ones they will take at the stated value, up to one-half the total value.

- **Alternating Method:** Both parties take turns choosing one community item at a time.

- **Equalizing Payment Method:** One party agrees to receive less property (furniture, dishes, and so on) in exchange for a payment from the other party.

- **Take-It-or-Leave-It Method:** One party places a value on an asset and the other party can either let the first party have the asset, or take it themselves as part of their share.

- **Appraise-It Method:** The parties choose an appraiser to value certain items. The parties then alternate selecting these items until they have acquired their share.

- **Closeout-Sale Method:** If there are items that cannot be agreed upon, sell the items and divide the proceeds to achieve an equal distribution.

- **The-Envelope-Please Method:** Each party enters a bid for particular items. Each bid is opened at the same time and the highest bidder gets the items. The item's dollar value is then added to the winning bidder's total.

Use Neutral Experts: The financial benefits of utilizing neutral experts, instead of battling these issues out in court, are obvious and can be substantial. When expert information or advice is needed in an adversarial divorce, each attorney hires an expert to issue an opinion, and, if necessary, testify in court. In the end, the couple pays for two expert opinions. When an expert is needed in mediation or some other alternative divorce process, the mediator or attorney may give the divorcing couple a few names. The couple interviews the experts and agrees on one they will mutually employ to give an opinion.

Different experts may be necessary depending on the subject area being discussed. For example, it is not unusual for an expert opinion to be necessary to appraise the marital and premarital portions of a retirement plan. Most people need to have their home appraised to determine the fair market value—asking their expert to give an honest, neutral value, neither high nor low. Sometimes an expert can give a range of value and clients can negotiate a fair value that they can both agree to.

Your Most Important Decision

You are about to embark on a series of decisions that will have the most significant emotional and financial impact of any decisions you have ever made in your life. Take your time to choose the right team to guide you and the right divorce option to follow. *And,* if you realize down the line that you have chosen the wrong professionals or the wrong option, cut your losses and find the right ones. Trust me, it will be worth it.

Conclusion

After my editor read this book, she said, "In my divorce, I did absolutely everything you say *not* to do." So I asked, "How did that turn out for you?" and she replied, "It was a lot tougher on all of us than it needed to be. If only I'd read this book before. . ."

I wish I could be with each and every one of you to provide my support and professional expertise in person as you move through your divorce. But that's physically impossible. So I gathered the best advice, insight and insider tips from my 20+ years of experience and put it all together for you in this book. I've also included websites and other resources for further information and wisdom.

Now it's up to you. You can apply what you learned in these pages, or put the book down and do your divorce the hard way. Divorce is not a walk in the park—but now you have some tools to make it easier if you choose to do so.

If you remember nothing else from this book, please remember these four key points:

1. **Take care of yourself**. By practicing self-care through eating well, exercising and getting enough rest, you will think more clearly and feel better which will enhance your ability to make the best possible decisions for yourself and your family.

2. **Learn to communicate in new ways**. Good communication is key to creating solutions and achieving mutually

acceptable outcomes. The tools offered in this book will help you learn to listen more fully and to express yourself so you can be heard. It takes some effort, but once you've mastered them, you'll find that good communication skills are valuable all areas of your life.

3. **Take your time**. You have many choices to make so take the time to make them mindfully. Avoid reacting out of hurt, fear, or anger. No matter what your choices or how you made them in the past, this is your opportunity to choose differently.

4. **Embrace the change**. Change is tough, but it's also the catalyst for growth and expansion. "When one door closes, another one opens" and that new open door can have exciting possibilities *if* you choose to view it that way. Your attitude about these changes, whether positive or negative, will be contagious and impact the entire process and its outcomes.

My sincere wish is that your divorce process is empowering, respectful and positions you for a fulfilling future. You can choose whether to make your divorce a devastating ordeal or a jumping off point for your new life. My hope for you is that this challenging process of divorce becomes an opportunity for you to grow and thrive.

ABOUT THE AUTHOR

Carol Delzer is a family law mediator and collaborative attorney with more than twenty years of experience working with divorcing couples and teaching co-parenting skills. In addition to being a Certified Family Law Specialist, certified by the State Bar of California, Delzer is a Licensed Marriage Family Therapist licensed by the California State Board of Behavioral Science. She has been a licensed California Real Estate Broker for over thirty years and is an experienced mindful negotiator.

Carol is President of Family Law Center in Sacramento, California, with a mission of providing a sensible, fair, compassionate, effective and affordable alternative to divorcing families. Where the motto is: "Divorce Done Differently."

It was through her divorce and being a single parent that Carol learned the importance of this work—divorce can be easier when couples are made aware of the options.

Delzer was one of the founding members of the Sacramento Collaborative Practice Group. She helped design, run and serve as a volunteer mediator for the California Superior Court Volunteer Mediation Program. Carol has served on numerous nonprofit boards and contributed countless volunteer hours to her community.

This is the third book she has written or co-authored. Her previous books are *Collaborative Co-parenting* published in 2009 and *Positive Discipline for Single Parents* which she co-authored with Jane Nelsen in 1995, now in its third edition.

To learn more about Carol, visit her websites: www. DivorceDoneEasier.com, www.FamilyLawCenter.US and www. CollaborativeCoParenting.com